THE GREAT
HIMALAYAN
TREASURE

THE GREAT HIMALAYAN TREASURE

ABOUT LIFE, BALANCE, AND SUCCESS!

VARUN WADHWA

Anecdote
Publishing House

Anecdote Publishing House
E-35-A, E Block, Gali No. 2 Ganesh Nagar,
Pandav Nagar Complex Delhi-110092

Published by Anecdote Publishing House
Copyright © Varun Wadhwa

First Edition 2022

ISBN 978-81-952518-9-6

MRP ₹ 399

All Rights Reserved.
No part of this publication may be reproduced, stored in a retrieval system, or transmitted in any form, or by any means—electronic, mechanical, photocopying, recording or otherwise—without the prior permission of the publisher. Opinions expressed in it are the author's own. The publisher is in no way responsible for these.

Book Promoted and Marketed by Champ Readers Pvt. Ltd.
Edited by Swati Vijay
Layout by Graphic Tailor
Printed by Thomson Press (India) Ltd, New Delhi

Dedicated to All the Seekers

Who settle for nothing less
than the truth!

To my family & friends
I love you!

CONTENTS

Introduction ix
Prologue xix

The Chamber 1
Blind Love 13
Work Is Worship 20
The Orange Sky 27
The Huddle 33
First Hurdle – The Chanting Saint 41
The Second Hurdle – Depth Of The Ocean 58
The Third Hurdle – Shangrila, The Hidden Waterfalls 80
Kailash – Journey To The Divine 105
The Final Destination 116
Balance Comes From Within! 132

Goodbye Message From The Author 179
Acknowledgements 203

INTRODUCTION

There have been people who have written about their success stories and there have been those who have written about their failures. Every story has imbibed learnings that are worth exploring, irrespective of the conclusion.

The Ramayana for instance was the most epic story which has been written or spoken about for thousands of years by the great saints and intellectuals. Lord Rama is worshipped not just in India but throughout the South Asian countries. Today also, when people talk about an ideal country, they refer to the 'Ram Rajya'. However, if you read about the life of Lord Rama, you would see that his life went through series of challenges. From being sent to the exile on account of two boons to Kaikeyi, to his beloved wife Sita being abducted by Ravana. Then fighting a bloody war to win her back only to again being forced to send her back to the jungle due to a political situation. Finally, in the end, fighting a battle with his sons and never seeing his wife and children again. If you would think through you would not call this a successful life, not as per the parameters of today's society. However, you must realize that irrespective of all these challenges, Lord Rama maintained his sense of balance and tranquillity. His sense of administration for his kingdom had been spoken about for centuries. These are the qualities we worship; these are the learnings we try to imbibe in our day-to-day life.

There would have been many stories that would have come your way through books, videos, movies, articles, serials, etc. The question is: Why should you read this story? What is so unique about the characters who are parts of this book?

Essentially everything about these characters would remind you about something in yourself, in a way they reflect the society that we all live in. The society that believes that being stressed by your job/ profession, showing anger towards your co-workers, having an occasional brawl in a nightclub, spending sleepless nights on account of a break up, dwelling about past failures for years, are all borderlines but accepted behaviours. A society that believes that personality is a permanent trait of behaviours that cannot be easily altered.

If you would search for the origin of the word personality this is what you would find:

'The word personality comes from the Latin word 'persona'. In the ancient world, a persona was a mask worn by an actor. While we tend to think of a mask as being worn to conceal one's identity, the theatrical mask was originally used to either represent or project a specific personality trait of a character.'

Thus, personality is not something you are born with; it is something that you acquire as you start to get conditioned first by your family, then by the society and at last with the people walk into your life that may be your teachers, friends, life partner, movie stars, mentors and even acquaintances. Therefore, we all have a choice; we can look to transform ourselves for the better by choosing to wear the mask that best serves our interests along with the interests of our loved ones but most importantly the one that serves the interests of this world in general.

However, the challenge is that far too many people believe that personalities are something you cannot change easily, you would have seen so many people who get angry too often, give themselves an excuse saying, 'This is who I am, what should I do'.

That's because people have spent decades on this planet and yet they have no control over their minds and emotions. My question is: Are you planning to learn this in another life or perhaps are you waiting for some magic to happen overnight wherein you get magically transformed into an ideal human being?

Well, let the truth be told, there is no magic wand that would suddenly transform us to an ideal state. In fact there are no ideal human beings in this world, we are all works in progress. Essentially there are only two categories of human beings if I think through these lines. Some have understood that our body and mind take instructions from them and then there are those who believe that they are controlled by these dimensions.

Therefore, to put it more precise there are more

evolved human beings and there are less evolved human beings.

You may question me saying that I am wrong; some ideal human beings walked this planet, those who embarked on this wonderful journey and left their mark to inspire many generations to come. The likes of Martin Luther King, Mahatma Gandhi, Nelson Mandela, Mother Teresa, Isaac Newton, Albert Einstein, etc., the list goes on.

And I would agree with you, that if you study their lives, you will consider them as close to an ideal human being. But most importantly, I think they were evolved human beings who had taken charge of their respective faculties.

If you are willing to invest too, you could transform into someone beautiful and there is a reason why I use that word. You see, society defines something as beautiful from what they generally see, therefore it's only a filtered version. There is beauty in all of us and everyone truly deserves to explore this side which makes them beautiful human beings.

Who should read this book?

There is something in this book for everyone; however, I have tried to list the people to whom this book is likely to appeal the most.

For a Student

If you are a student, this book could help you to see a new light across the tunnel when it comes to positive cavalries, it may perhaps enlighten you with creative ideas about the next steps in your journey.

In my own experience, I have observed far too many students feel lost in their professional and personal journey, looking for answers to the thousands of questions that have been going around in their heads. Something that I struggled too in my younger days. This book tries to answer the primary question which may be spinning inside your head:

Where do I go from here?

In my experience as a professional trainer and consultant, I have seen that many graduates simply have no clue in which direction they should take their careers. Most of them rely on guidance from their parents, relatives and friends to tell them what's good for them. Most often they receive advice that channelizes their energy into a profession that is most popular during those times. A few years earlier it was chartered accountancy, nowadays it's artificial intelligence.

But if you are a student who is reading this, it's always worthwhile for you to explore the whole idea behind what it means to live a successful life. Far too many students have embodied a flawed definition of success which they have caught on from the society, a society that only measures success by the money that you have in your bank account. Therefore, many students get into a field of study which seemed lucrative at that time; however, they later resent their decisions. This book may not give you any insights about which field to choose but would certainly help you ensure that you give your hundred percent no matter which field you choose and be joyful in the process which is not such a bad deal!

For a Professional

If you are a professional who is stuck in your career or you would like to make the most of your time at work, the book could be a cornerstone from where your life simply takes the right turn. Salaried professionals often question if they are being paid enough and start blaming their industry, their company, their bosses and the economy. Business professionals on the other hand often blame the prevailing market conditions, their competition, not having enough finance, good partners, family support, etc.

The book hopefully would help you at least reach one empowering decision in your head that could alter your professional life completely: 'Whether you make it in life it's you, whether you don't make it in life it's you.'

This is important because far too many people have got away in this world by blaming something or someone for their failures. You should not be one of those! This simple idea moves you away from a victim mentality to a winner mentality. And winners while they may have many qualities which take them forward, all of them have a thing in common whether they realize it or not: A certain sense of balance!

For a Parent

I am a parent myself and I know when it comes to our children every parent is concerned about the unwanted outside influence that could potentially pollute the mind of the young ones. While we empower our little ones with the best of education and facilities, we often don't pay enough attention to understand their learning and influence patterns.

A child would naturally first look up to you for inspiration, however, he/she would only feel inspired if you have taken charge of your own life. If you are somehow going through life haphazardly, just looking to survive the daily chores, then stress, fear, anger, frustration, and anxiety are a natural happening. Now imagine a child whose natural state is joy and happiness witnessing all these anomalies. How do you think he/she would be able to relate with you? Naturally, the child would look for inspiration outside the four walls and there goes your opportunity of positively influencing your child and showing them the right direction. In my view, the best gift you could give your loved ones including your child is to be the best version of yourself.

But coming back to the point, the power we have over our children in terms of shaping their future is immense, so if you are looking to create a legacy that truly lasts beyond your lifetime, this book is for you!

For a Seeker

A seeker for me stands above everyone, not in stature but in relentlessness for he/she shall never compromise on their path to wisdom, he/she shall not be content with anything apart from truth itself. For there is no bigger solace than the truth, there is no bigger religion than the truth and there is no bigger authority than the truth. In fact 'Truth is the only authority.'

For all the fellow seekers out there, this is a small but genuine attempt to throw some light into the path of darkness which eclipse all of us as we start our spiritual journey. People often perceive spirituality as a journey and start searching for a destination which they like to name enlightenment. Whereas for me spirituality has been like a vehicle on which I could sail through the ups and downs of life without feeling distressed.

When my dad passed away, I knew it was going to be the biggest test for my resilience. He was a great influence in my life and saying goodbye wasn't easy. There were so many things which I wanted to tell him including how much I loved him; however, a letter was all I could write which I placed near his body on his last journey. On the third day of his funeral rights, I had my conference in Singapore. I knew if I would not go, everybody would understand. There was chaos outside, however, within me I was peaceful and serene. I had realized that there are only two ways that you could deal with the loss of a loved one. Either accept that situation with grace or make chaos out of it. Accepting this with grace gave me the opportunity to find a solution instead of searching for solace. In case you are wondering if I did attend the Singapore conference, then yes indeed I did. I would always miss him but finding solace in this pain isn't the solution. You must look for opportunities to grow through each of these unfortunate events.

For now, just understand this much, that we cannot choose the situations that life throws at us, we can only and only choose our response. The book attempts to help you respond consciously to these situations as they come along. Also, as a fellow seeker, I hope you find answers to some of the other most burning questions about life through this book.

Let's Start!

For anything good to happen to you, the first and foremost thing is that you must be receptive to everything. If you keep looking upwards praying for only the good things to happen to you, then you would simply miss the experience, miss the amazing phenomenon called life. When it rains some people take shelter while others simply enjoy the weather. A farmer may be rejoicing these rains whereas some businessman who is stuck in traffic would be cursing them. Does this mean that the farmer is right, and the businessman is wrong? Well, not really, this simply means that we must learn to embrace every situation which comes along our way, just the way it is, without attaching any unnecessary meaning.

Embracing this life just the way it is, presents you with the opportunity to think clearly, and with clarity comes sound decision making. We all know that we are where we are because of the decisions that we have taken in our life. With a different decision, we would have landed someplace else. If I would like to attach an equation to this point, it would look something like this:

Embracing situations | Clarity | Sound Decision Making | Right Actions | Required Outcome

If I were simply reverse this equation then we would need to simply understand that if you would like to have the required outcomes in your life, you must learn to embrace every situation just the way it is. Being receptive and growing through every life situation is a capability that only a human being possesses. The words that I have used to describe the book include life, balance, and success but there is one word missing which is the underlying theme that runs through the book, and that one word is 'journey'.

A journey that all the characters in this book undertake and the journey we all must undertake to become a little more than we are today.

But Varun, Hey I came for the treasure hunt, what's with all these learnings?

Well, if you came for the thrill of the treasure hunt, I bet you would be entertained, the learning is the icing on the cake for every experience you have must grow you in some manner, which includes the experience of reading this book.

So now are you ready to begin this journey?

PROLOGUE

The Year 548 CE
Somewhere in the Himalayas!

It was a cold chilly morning as a hundred men stood there with their armour's surrounding and protecting the chests which were kept in the lap of the Himalayas. The bone-chilling winds were enough to kill any human being within a few moments; however, these men were brave as they stood for their empire, for their king, and for their treasure.

For one whole year they had scaled through the forests, the rivers, climbed up the many mountain scales to find the perfect place which matched their king's description to bury this treasure.

The king had instructed them, 'Our Empire is crumbling, as humble servants to this empire which you have served for many years; it is your duty to protect this treasure from the enemies. A treasure of this scale and magnitude must not fall into the hands of our enemies.

With the constant attacks from the Huns as well as the rise of the Vakataks as well as the Yashodharaman empires, it is unlikely we would survive another blow.

This heavenly treasure should be preserved at the hands of the almighty until someone who is the child of God, could discover it and rightfully bestow it for the benefit of humanity.'

Vishnugupta who was the last of the Gupta kings wanted to survey the place himself before he could instruct his ministers to bury the treasure. For the one last time, he looked at the heavenly treasure as he nodded in affirmation towards his ministers.

He then gazed towards the mountains as he remembered the glory of his forefathers which had ruled this land for many years before him. He was proud of their legacy, proud of their military might, and for their contributions to science, art, and literature. The period gave rise to many significant accomplishments in architecture, sculpture, music, and painting that set standards of form and taste that were going to be revered for many centuries to come. The whole endeavour completely altered the course of political administration, not only in India but far beyond her borders.

The time period which has since been known as 'The Golden Age of India'

CHAPTER 1

THE CHAMBER

The year 2021
Somewhere in the Himalayas!

This was their sixth expedition in as many years in search of the grand treasure for which they had heard very little about.

'Are you sure the treasure is for real, I am beginning to have my doubts,' said Leena looking suspiciously towards Raman as the two made their way back to the place down the slope where they had parked their car.

'So far we have only heard about the treasure from professor, it does not find a reference anywhere else where I have read, so I am not sure either,' replied Raman.

'Maybe we should take a break and do something else for a while, we have given six years of our lives to this treasure hunt without any material returns, my parents are started to think that I am some idiot who is wasting her time,' added Leena.

'Have you told them about the treasure?' enquired

Raman as he looked at Leena who looked beautiful and attractive, as she washed her face.

Leena gave Raman that look, and he figured out that he had asked a stupid question. Leena was a history student, who had an inquisitive style for things, coming from a small town, she was all beautiful, elegant and tomboyish in her jeans as well as in black overcoat. She wasn't the showstopper, but she was sure to get noticed whichever room she entered.

Raman on the other hand was a tall and thin young man, affable but certainly not charming.

He came from a family of treasure hunters starting with his grandfather; however, their legacy was anything but great. He had that bewildered look about him, always searching for answers.

Though together they looked like a team and had a warm understanding between them, Raman had a secret crush on Leena, however, she hardly paid any attention to him.

As they made their way near the car, Raman could sense that something was wrong. The rear driver-side door of the car was open.

'Someone has forced open the car, come quickly,' Raman said as he ran the last few steps towards the car.

'The map, it's gone, the professor would kill us and bury us in the chambers,' remarked Raman in a tone which had a sense of both frustration as well as fear.

'Where did you keep the map?' asked Leena.

'In the front drawer, it's not there anymore,' replied Raman still looking for it everywhere in the car as well as his pockets.

'Did you see someone following us?' asked Leena.

'No one that I can remember, but what should we do now?' enquired Raman in a tensed tone.

'We have to inform the professor, I am calling him,' mentioned Leena.

Leena went about calling the professor as Raman enquired from the nearby shops about the thief. They had parked the car somewhere near the market but just far enough, so no one really notices.

'Nobody has seen or heard anything, not even the noise of the glass being broken,' said Raman as he hit the top of the car with his fist in anger.

'What did the professor say?' asked Raman after a couple of minutes.

'Well you know him, Raman, he is a man of few words, he asked us to come back' replied Leena.

'Did he sound upset?' asked Raman.

'We would find out, I guess,' replied Leena.

***

3 Hours Earlier

'We must hurry up; we need to get our marked point before it gets dark. Who knows what lies ahead?' remarked Raman.

'Stop behaving like a little girl, would you?' replied Leena.

'I am not,' added Raman.

'Yes, you are and if you are so damn afraid then you should have taken up a regular office job, who asked you to become a treasure hunter like your forefathers?' she continued.

'Will you shut up and drive the car?' said Raman looking frantically in the rear mirror to make sure that no one was following them.

'And will you please sit back and relax, no one is following us. You are making me nervous,' said Leena giving Raman an angry look.

'Alright let's park here, our marked point is about 4-5 km walking from here on that trail,' said Leena showing Raman the shortcut, which went through the forests.

'Yes, that's what the Shepherd also told us I guess' replied Raman as they got out of the car.

As they marched forward, the road had a craggy coastline with a narrow dusty path.

They would have travelled for about 2 km when they saw a scenic village, which was surrounded by undulating hills. Meanwhile, a landscape with bigger hills – mountains looked over the village at a distance; it was a snow-capped mountain range. Everywhere they looked it was rolling hills.

'We should settle down here,' said Raman.

'Absolutely, but not with a little girl like you,' tinkered Lenna.

'Come on, I would cook food for you every day,' added Raman with a smile on his face.

'Focus on the task in hand, otherwise, the professor would rip us apart,' replied Leena.

'Why are you so afraid of the professor?' asked Raman.

'Our report card shows that we have failed for the last

six years, do you need another reason?' answered Leena as she stopped and looked at Raman.

'So I am not afraid of the professor but I know that he could go to any length to find this treasure and if we continue to disappoint him, it would not be long before his patience runs out,' explained Leena.

'Let's hope this expedition leads to at least one of the clues to the treasure,' replied Raman staring at the steep climb that lay ahead.

As they were nearing their destination a sense of anxiety was running in their head.

'Is this the cave we were referring to?' asked Raman as they climbed for about 2 km more. On the one side of the cave was an old deserted house that stood on a bleak hilltop.

'Yes, this is our place, the cave's mouth should be on the other side of the hill,' said Leena sounding excited.

The mouth of the cave appeared like a welcoming blue eye. All around the cave, the mountains were covered with a rug of trees, green, yellow, scarlet and orange, but their bare tops were scarfed and beribboned with snow. From carved rocky outcrops, waterfalls drifted like skeins of white lawn, and in the fields, they could see the amber glint of rivers and the occasional mirror-like flash of a mountain lake.

As they entered the boundary between light and dark, they hesitated for a while since their heart was thumping. From the overhead clumps of moss, cold drops plopped into their hair, a water clock ticking away the precious seconds. Then there was a musty smell coming.

'That smell and noise, is it coming from bats?' asked

Raman as he put on his torchlight from the phone.

The cave did not have a large boundary and soon the two of them found themselves at the end of a rocky trail with no way forward.

Raman looked around everywhere and signalled to Leena that he had not found anything.

'There is nothing here, just some old rocks, we have been wrong again about the clues,' said Leena as she sat in one of those rocks looking frustrated and tired. Raman too came out after searching frantically inside the cave.

'The village would come again on our way back, my proposal is still open,' mentioned Raman trying to cheer her up.

Leena didn't say anything as she gave Raman a cold look and started her climb back from the mountain top.

As they made their climb down, two shadows appeared from behind the old deserted house and stood out looking at the two treasure hunters.

They were dressed in a black robe from head to toe with their head covered with a black cloth tied up. The only thing which was visible was their almond-shaped eyes, with eyelids that didn't have a crease as well as hooded lids that drooped somewhat over the eyes. Those eyes had vigour and purpose, the eyes of the assassins. For someone looking at them, they reminded of the 'Black Ninjas.'

One of them took a semiautomatic handgun and aimed at the two treasure hunters. The other man stopped his hand before he could shoot.

'NOT YET, THEY ARE JUST KIDS' said the man with a heavy voice as the two men stood there looking down. One of them took out the map and burned it with a lighter as ashes flew in the air.

***

Society of Ancient India – The Chamber Room

There was little to say as the professor looked into the eyes of his disciples searching for answers, however, all he could find was despair and repentance.

The professor was a short and clumsy guy. His eyes were gentle, had a soft beard, a tailored suit, and a classic spectacle. He was someone who had exceptional knowledge on the treasure, having spent the majority of his life towards this endeavour. From his mannerism, he appeared to be someone who had a deep understanding of human psychology.

They were sitting in a private chamber where the society members would conduct business not required to be brought in open court.

The society was formed with the objective of exploring the culture and heritage of ancient India, primarily the stone implements and cave paintings from this period which were discovered in many parts of South Asia. There were also studies performed on evidence of domestication of animals, the adoption of agriculture, permanent village settlements and wheel-turned pottery. The professor taught this subject in the history class in various colleges in Delhi.

He had been appointed as the chair to the society around ten years back and ever since that he had been secretly utilizing the resources of the society to find any information that he could on the Great Himalayan Treasure.

'It's been thirty-eight years since I started on this journey to find the treasure, with very little help or resources. After so much effort and hard work you are telling me that someone stole that map from your car. The map which was only left clue that we had which could have paved the way for us to search for the next links,' roared the professor.

He stopped for a moment as he recollected his teenage days when his grandfather who had brought him up had handed over the keys to him of the hidden room in his house where he had collected all the information about the treasure.

'The treasure that is being talked about in ancient books is not a myth my son, it is for real and I want you to find it,' said the grandfather.

Those were his last words as the professor now well into his late fifties had grown up with the dream of someday finding the treasure. He did not marry nor had any children since his only real motive was to find the hidden treasure. His great grandfather who had led a secretive life did not allow his grandson to notice anything that would suggest that he was a treasure hunter until he was on his deathbed. The professor also knew he had to carry out his work secretly since the treasure was too big and would warrant unwanted attention.

He had only disclosed his secret to his two disciples who worked closely with him for the last many years. While the professor was always certain that there must be someone else as well who would be after this treasure, his hesitation now became certain with the map being stolen from the car.

'You were right professor, we are not alone in this treasure hunt, someone else is also after that and we don't know how powerful they are,' said Raman in a fearful voice.

'That's not my worry,' said the professor.

'Nobody knows more than us about this treasure, and without that knowledge, that map is useless, though you should have been more careful with that map' continued the professor.

'You have taught us well professor, how you expect that we would make that novice mistake,' said Leena as she looked at the professor.

'The map that those thieves stole from our car was only a replica of the actual map, the original is still lying here in the chamber in our safe room,' remarked Leena proudly.

Leena opened the drawer at the professor's desk and pulled the hidden lever which was situated just below the desk. The door situated at the side of the library room moved just enough for anyone to pass through.

It was a small safe room that the professor had built along with his two disciples many years ago, it was a room that none of the other society members were aware of. All the material which was kept in the professor's home had been shifted to this safe room as the professor suspected that someone was watching his home constantly. This was after his home had been burgled in the middle of the night, however, the thieves had to return empty-handed since none of the jewels or cash was stolen. The professor was certain that the thieves had come to steal information about the treasure.

After long contemplation, he had taken the decision to move all these belongings to the society chamber. He had figured that no one would suspect that this information was lying at his chamber office. Most of this information included books and diaries which the professor's grandfather had maintained detailing his expeditions into the great Himalayas in search of the treasure. Well, it wasn't much since he was no closer to the treasure on his last day than he was when he started, but it was all the professor had.

The professor had added his own research into this treasure hunt which was all kept at the safe room in the society chambers.

As the three entered the safe room, Leena took out the map from one of the small cupboards in the safe room. The professor was both relieved and happy to see the map which he had received as perhaps the most important possession from his grandfather.

His grandfather never discussed this treasure hunt with

his grandchild, so he wasn't even sure if the map was real.

'We need to go back to the drawing board professor, we have made very little progress in the expeditions that we have made to the Himalayas,' said Raman.

'He is right professor and now more than ever we need to move fast since someone else apart from us also has that map,' added Leena.

'Yes, both of you are right; we must progress quickly before someone else finds the next clue to this treasure. Let's take all the important information from this safe room and sit in the main chamber room. Today is Tuesday and none of the society members are expected to visit the office,' mentioned the professor as he started to move out of the secret room.

'Why didn't you tell me that you had the map,' said Raman nudging Leena.

'I wanted to see my little girl cry,' replied Leena with a grin on her face.

CHAPTER II

BLIND LOVE

Amar looked out of his car window at the child who stood outside his car asking for money. He rolled down his window shades not to offer him anything but rather to abuse him for spoiling his mood.

'Get out from my site, every day the same thing,' he shouted. The small child was tantalized as he ran towards his mother, who started her hurls of abuse towards Amar. He cared the least as the traffic light turned green.

Amar had been late again to the office as he hurried from parking towards the office reception. The receptionist smiled at Amar as always but he was in no mood to return that smile as usual as he signed on the official register. The receptionist whispered to her friend as Amar got into the office:

'Such a hunk, why doesn't he ever pay attention to me?'

'He is married, and you know it, what do you expect,' replied her friend.

'Only a smile would do for me,' said the receptionist

with anticipation in her voice, looking at the office door from Amar had just entered the office.

Amar was an ex-Mr India runner-up, though he was still in the prime of his health, he was full of envy for not winning the title.

He had made grand plans of going on to compete for the Mr World title and starting his modelling career in the industry. Those disappointing moments having unfortunately stayed with him for long. Though it had been eight long years ever since he lost the title, Amar was finding it hard to move on with his life.

He had married with his childhood friend Neha and together they had a four-year-old boy named Kabir. They had made their home in Bangalore, although from the last few months her wife along with his son had gone back to Chandigarh.

While the first couple of years were great for both of them, ever since then the two had been having bitter arguments over almost anything.

Amar had settled down in a quiet job in the learning and development industry where he would train the people about physical fitness. During weekends he would work as a consultant in the nearby health club. There were rumours of him asking girls out at the health club for dates even though he had never been caught, however, Neha constantly kept hearing these rumours from her friends.

Last year, when she finally chose to confront Amar on this issue, he struck it down as if it's nothing. But wives generally get the vibe when their husbands are not being truthful to them, it is some kind of sixth sense that they have. Neha knew that Amar was hiding something; however, she could not exactly pinpoint it.

Neha who was also a volunteer in a spiritual organization even tried to convince Amar to join so that they could spend some time together. She had also seen the remarkable change this volunteering work has bought about in her approach towards life in the last year. Even though Amar was hardly there for her giving her any emotional support, she had not lost hope or become negative. All she ever wanted was for her husband to be there for her, however, she could see that there was a clear lack of emotional support on his part.

Three months ago, when Amar came home one night from his office, Neha had been waiting for long. When Amar entered the room, he did not pay attention to Neha and headed straight to the room to change.

Neha who was already enraged couldn't hold herself anymore as she shouted:

'I have been waiting for you for the last four hours, where have you been? You haven't even cared to pick up my calls.'

Amar who looked visibly in a bad mood replied: 'I am not in the mood to argue tonight, we would speak tomorrow.'

Neha's outrage grew as she said: 'both I and Kabir were waiting to have dinner with you. When you were late, I made him eat, but I haven't eaten since then. Do you even care?'

'Did I ask you to wait for me, next time please have your dinner,' Amar said in a straightforward voice.

'But I am asking, where were you?' asked Neha.

'I went to a friend's place after my gym training,' replied Amar.

'You could have at least told me, I would not be worried, it's a reasonable demand I suppose,' asked Neha.

'Do I need to tell you everything, stop pretending to be my mother' shouted Amar.

'I am not being your mother, but I am your wife after all and I was waiting for dinner,' replied Neha.

'You heard me, don't wait next time,' said Amar.

'Sure, I won't but please go and tell your son whom you had promised that you would take him his friend's place tonight, how many more promises would you forget Amar,' replied Neha.

'I would take him tomorrow, please don't make an issue out of every damn thing and I would do whatever I like, don't you dare question,' shouted Amar as he raised his finger towards Neha.

Neha was quiet as she stepped out of the hall where the two were arguing. She quietly went to her son's bedroom where he had been sleeping peacefully unaware of the storm that had been brewing amongst his parents.

That had been the tipping point for Neha as the next morning she had gone along with his son to their parents' house.

The next morning when he got up to see if Neha was asleep in his son's room, he could not find them anywhere.

When he called his Neha's number it was switched off, it was only later that evening that Amar's father-in-law called him to inform that Neha and Kabir were at their place in Chandigarh.

'Please ask them never to come back,' shouted Amar to his father-in-law as he kept the phone down.

Many days had passed since then, even though Amar did miss his family, he had too much self-pride to extend a warm hand to his wife asking for forgiveness.

It was a Sunday afternoon as Amar's phone rang. Expecting it to be Neha's call, he got off the bed excited to pick up the phone. It wasn't Neha but rather Nishant, his childhood friend.

'Hi Nishant, how are you doing?' said Amar in a less exciting voice.

'Hello, aren't you excited to hear my voice after so long?' asked Nishant.

'Nothing, I was just expecting Neha's call, she is away at her parents' house,' replied Amar.

'So, you miss them, my baby boy,' mentioned Nishant.

'Nothing like that, you tell me, what new have you discovered in your surveys,' asked Amar.

'Listen if Neha and Kabir are away then that's good news because I had a great travel offer for "The Himalayan Resort, Uttarakhand." Are you interested?' asked Nishant.

Amar wasn't too sure but Nishant insisted: 'Come on, Rahul may join us too, this is a great opportunity to revive some of the old college days when the three of us hung out.'

Amar thought to himself, yea why not, it's good way to take my mind away from my screwed-up personal life.

'Alright count me in,' replied Amar.

THE FIRST DIMENSION: BODY

People over the ages have been fascinated with the idea of living forever or searching for the fountain of youth. The legend says that Alexander the emperor went to great lengths in search for a magical well from where he could drink water and become immortal.

The history of the human race is filled with enumerable examples of people looking to explore ways to keep this body in good health for they know that this is the only place they have to live.

This body has been described as our home and if you read the scriptures, they have asked you to keep it clean as a temple. This doesn't simply mean that we keep it cleanse from the outside, it means we genuinely take care of it as if our life depends on it, and the truth be told, our life does depend on it. People, however, at times go to the extreme and start identifying too much with their bodies. Their excuse is that the body has its own needs, i.e. the need for sex, food and pleasure.

Sex in the body is fine; the problem starts when it reaches your head. Then, it becomes a compulsive behaviour that you cannot get rid of even though you have tried. Far too many youngsters today face this challenge that they simply cannot focus on their studies or job because their head is spinning with falsified ideas about sex and romance.

Similarly, trying new cuisines to satisfy your taste buds is fine; the problem starts when you start romanticizing with food. In the most pragmatic sense food is nothing but means of nourishment for this body, just like all machines need fuel to give them energy, so does our body. Therefore, trying to identify which food is best for nourishment is not a difficult job, all it requires is some common sense.

Now everyone knows it's imperative that we look after our body, so we could stay fit and healthy for as long as possible. Also, everyone wants to die while they are still living an active social life and self-reliant. However, the guidance we receive regarding body care is contradictory and often baffling for a variety of motives:

i. The food advertisement industry which constantly feeds us information every day does not want us to eat healthily; all they care is about their sales numbers. The question is, how do we look beyond these advertisements?

ii. Personal health is not a zero-sum game which means there is no one means to achieve good health. Therefore, it often becomes a challenge to know to whom we should follow. Especially since there are multiple sources through which we receive information and whoever we listen to calls themselves an expert in this field. So, who should be that authority in our lives to whom you must look up to while making these decisions?

iii. Also like I said there is no one single path to personal health, from exercise to running, to morning walks, to yoga, to dancing, virtually all of these have been associated with personal health. So, how do we decide which one is most effective and gives healthier results?

iv. Every food has its nourishment qualities, how does one decide which food is best for our body?

v. With a constant influx of movies, videos, and the entire entertainment industry which uses sexual desires as a means to sell more content, how does one not allow all of these to distract ourselves from our path to greater fulfillment?

vi. Major reason for couples separating is because one of them cheated in their relationship. Having multiple partners has become the norm rather than an exception in today's society, the challenge is how does one overcome these relationship challenges?

The answer to all of the above questions could be possibly accessed if we understand a little more about the word: Balance!

We shall talk more about it later but for now, let's move on.

CHAPTER III

WORK IS WORSHIP

Nishant had been thinking about this for long, he could not even remember the last time he took a break from his work to spend some quality time with his family and friends.

Aryan, his son had once again walked into his laboratory only to find out that his dad had been busy doing some science work. It was a typical Delhi weekend, where Nishant had promised his son that they would go out for the latest *Avengers movie, which had just hit the theatres.*

Nishant was a scientist but also did archaeology, which his family never really understood.

Nishant would try to explain to them, 'Archaeological science, also known as archaeometry, consists of the application of scientific techniques to the analysis of archaeological materials, to assist in dating the materials. Thus, am an actual scientist, I am not making things up for the sake of it'.

Everyone would listen patiently and then return

to usual behind-the-back jokes about Nishant and his obsession with being called a scientist.

That day when Aryan walked back to his house from Nishant's private laboratory which he had set up in his garden, Isha was pissed off. She had been supportive of her husband's choice of career and his long hours of work which he spent away from his family members, but she was starting to lose her patience.

She held Aryan's hand as she took him back to the laboratory to confront Nishant, who was on an office call. He worked at the Archaeological Survey of India, Delhi.

Isha who had now become wiser in dealing with her husband's work habits waited patiently for the call to finish.

Finally, she spoke, 'I thought you were going to take him for the movie today, wasn't it supposed to be dad weekend?'

'Yea Isha I know that I had promised him but there is something which has come up for which my team needs some urgent help. You won't believe what the team at Patna has found,' replied Nishant.

Nishant was about to finish the sentence when Isha intervened, 'look Nishant, look at our faces, are these the faces of two people who care about what your team found in Patna or anywhere else. I am sure it's remains of some lost civilization or maybe you found some dead mummies who started walking as soon as you dug them out but for the last time, we don't care.' Isha looked at Aryan who was having a good laugh.

'What are you laughing at, this is not the movie you are supposed to be seeing,' said Isha looking at Aryan.

Then turning towards Nishant she said, 'Look Nishant while I understand that all that is important for you, but you must also think about what is important for your son.'

'Dead mummies you meant?' replied Nishant as he giggled and gave a high five to Aryan.

'Look this isn't funny, what would he do with your survey findings, can he play with those stones and coins that you keep researching over in your laboratory,' said Isha in a frustrated tone.

'Isha what do I do if this discovery came over the weekend, they are sending me some photographs which I need to review,' replied Nishant.

'But dad what about the movie?' asked Aryan who loved his dad for what he did but was looking forward to this movie.

'Aryan, I would take you next weekend, it's the most anticipated movie, it won't come out so soon from the theatres,' said Nishant looking at his son.

'Yea exactly, the most anticipated movie,' said Aryan as he simply walked out of the laboratory as this was not the first time that he had heard those kinds of words from his father. Isha followed her son after giving that split-second look to Nishant which suggested that he was not going to get any lunch or dinner today.

Nishant was usually alright with the arrangement since he anyways wasn't always concerned about food when he was doing a review on an important discovery. During such time the whole day would pass before he even realized that he had not eaten anything. Otherwise, though he was a foodie, who found it tough to keep his hands off any kind of food, which was served to him.

Though Nishant, was always a workaholic, but he had become even more so in the recent past, which had also taken a toll on his health. From high blood pressure to sugar, he had an entire menu that was dedicated to him because of his over-indulgence in his work along with his eating habits.

Most of the Zomato and Swiggy delivery guys who operated in his area had now saved his number given the frequent visits they had made to his residence. But health was least of the concern that bothered Nishant who happened to be a school as well as a college topper and had always been fascinated with Archaeological science. He remembered his father who was also fond of the subject but never found any time to dedicate to his passion since he was too busy supporting his family.

Thanks to his unhealthy lifestyle while his professional career had gone upwards along with his weight, his health deteriorated alongside the hair on his head.

That was going to be another long day for Nishant in his laboratory and even though Aryan, as well as Isha, were pissed off by Nishant's decision that day, he didn't care much. He expected that his family would understand that his work meant everything to him and would always take priority over everything else.

However, lately Nishant was starting to feel a little stressed out since his health was not supporting him and he had spent the entire week in the hospital three months ago recovering from his high blood pressure and diabetes alongside other health complications.

A couple of weeks later when he heard about the offer to travel to the Himalayan resort, Nishant sensed the perfect opportunity to take a break from his long working schedule. Isha was more than happy that his husband was finally taking a break as Nishant picked up the phone to call Amar and Rahul.

THE SECOND DIMENSION: MIND

The thing that everyone wants to change, is the way they think. People look at motivational books for solutions, they listen to saints and preachers for solace and often even go to quiet places to take a break from all that is going inside their heads.

The kind of research which has been done in the last fifty years to understand the human mind is fascinating. We can boast about being the generation that knows more about the human mind than any other previous generations did. Research especially in the field of neuroscience has been fascinating. Neuroscientists focus on the brain and its impact on behaviour and cognitive functions. Neuroscience is not only concerned with the normal functioning of the nervous system, but also what happens to the nervous system, when people have neurological, psychiatric and neurodevelopmental disorders.

Ask neuroscientists to define the area that they are studying, and one is bound to get a different answer every time. No longer fitting into one niche, the field can delve into the microcosm of molecules and cells but also expand out into the macrocosm of mankind itself. For example, did you know that an electrical implant can restore walking in paralysed patients or an adult human brain can produce new neurons until the tenth decade of life which means that you can still be as mentally as productive during the old age as you were during your youth? Our fascination with the mind however, is largely restricted to the human brain and if you are interested to know some interesting facts about our brain then here are some1:

- The human brain weighs 3 pounds.
- It comprises 60% of fat and is one of the fattest organs in the human body.
- Of the total blood and oxygen that is produced in our body, the brain gets 20% of it.
- When the blood supply to the brain stops, it is almost after 8-10 seconds that the brain starts losing consciousness.

- The brain is capable of surviving for 5 to 6 minutes only if it doesn't get oxygen after which it dies.
- The blood vessels that are present in the brain are almost 100,000 miles in length.
- There are 100 billion neurons present in the brain.

Experts say that the quality of the choices we make is dependent on the way we think. The kind of thoughts we have about the people around us, what we think about ourselves, and our thoughts about what we want to accomplish with our life all work together to form a way of living that governs our life and the choices that we make. In other words, the whole process of living starts in your head. Research shows that our thoughts are programming our lives at the rate of 1300 to 1800 words per minute, 24 hours a day, it is extremely important what kind of thoughts we allow in our minds.

The entire movie Matrix is dedicated to the idea that what we think about is directly correlated to the experiences that we subsequently encounter in our lives, the idea that the real world is an illusion.

According to Bob Proctor 'thoughts become things. If you see it in your mind, you will hold it in your hand, and if a person takes control over their mind, they then take control over their relationships, their wealth, their health, and everything. We are a group of people who have been trained and programmed to react to life rather than respond to life'.

The reason I am putting all these fascinating facts and findings out there for you to absorb is that I want you to understand that despite all these discoveries about our minds and thoughts, we still haven't reached a space where we have been able to transform these discoveries into tools of human wellbeing. A large part of our population still struggles with how to deal with the human mind. It's sad that this mind which has taken millions of years of evolution to reach space where it is right now, for most people it has become their worst nightmare.

One of the reasons that has happened is because while there are many different forms of intelligence which the human beings possess, our society only chooses to focus on memory. Please have a look at the way we have designed our education systems, it appears the ones that could memorize the most, are tagged as the most intelligent ones.

In school and college, we were asked to mug up the syllabus as we prepared for our exams, the ones that could remember the most were deemed to be intelligent while others were treated as if they came from some third-world nations. I still remember some of my friends who often came in the latter half of the class, were often given a hard time with their respective parents. And now when I meet them, they seem to be doing great in their respective fields.

I can recollect an incident where one of the most intelligent girls in our class was given a special red coat as a token of her achievement. We called her a study freak because we would see her studying while others were having their lunch during recess. It was one of those assembly days when she left her coat in the class. When we came back, we saw the coat hanging by the fan, somebody who was jealous of her achievement had gone bonkers and done that. Well, we never found out who was behind that horrible act, however, the point being that there is such a deep divide in society on this issue of intelligence vs memory.

While we would talk about this more later, for now, let's keep our focus on some of the most burning issues which concern the majority when it comes to them taking charge of their mind. If you were to ask people about their struggles, these are some of the responses you are likely to hear:

- My mind seems to have a mind of its own; it seems to do its own thing.
- Whenever I sit for meditation or try to focus on something, my mind wanders off in a different direction.
- Once I start with a negative chain of thought, I cannot let go. I get drowned and overwhelmed with these thoughts.
- I sometimes get a feeling that my mind is playing tricks with me; I cannot seem to control it.
- The more I do not want to think about something, the more I end up thinking about it. E.g., I recently broke up with my girlfriend and I do not want to think about her, but her thought always stays with me.
- I am so much intellectually drawn towards the work that I seem to forget everything. It's a great feeling because I feel I am in a flow; however, my personal life suffers immensely in the process.
- I tried thinking positive thoughts, but nothing transpired in my real life, what do I do?

And I repeat myself, the answer to all of the above questions or struggles could be possibly accessed if we understand a little more about the word: Balance!

Let's keep the ball rolling.

Notes:

Neuroscience Discoveries
https://singularityhub.com/2019/01/17/5-discoveries-that-made-2018-a-huge-year-for-neuroscience/
https://www.technologynetworks.com/neuroscience/lists/top-10-neuroscience-news-stories-of-2019-328615
https://www.sciencefirst.com/10-interesting-facts-about-the-human-brain/
https://www.learn-to-read-prince-george.com/thinking.html

CHAPTER IV

THE ORANGE SKY

Rahul was watching Bruno play in the garden as he sat there gazing at the beautiful orange evening sky. It was a Golden Retriever whom he had got five years back and it had become his most beloved friend. It was his birthday, however, he wanted to spend it alone.

Rahul worked as a marketing consultant at a start-up that had its office setup near Nehru Place in Delhi. He had grown up in Jaipur but had moved to Delhi ever since his parents decided to separate. For the first couple of years, he had stayed with each of his parents for six months each on rotation. But after a while, he was tired of these stints and decided to move to Delhi to stay alone and enjoy his independence. His mom would often visit him at his tiny apartment which he had taken in Kalkaji.

Rahul loved living with his partner Bruno who was probably his only sole companion who had stayed with him throughout his adult life.

Rahul, however, did miss not having anyone special in

his life to share his thoughts and feelings. He had a crush on his office colleague Kriti but never really dared to ask her out for a date even though he could feel the vibes between them whenever they were around. When Kriti first turned up in the office, almost everyone tried their luck except for Rahul who seemed more interested in talking to her about their marketing projects. She had even asked if he was interested in going out for a coffee, but Rahul was just too afraid to commit.

Finally, Kriti accepted the proposal of their marketing partner, however, she was still in some way waiting for Rahul to decide on her offer. However, Rahul for what had happened in his past was unlikely to make any commitments going forward. In his college days, he was seeing a girl who had ditched him to go out with his friend, and ever since then, Rahul was too afraid to fall in love again. He still remembered how hard it had been for him those initial days just as he had broken up with hardly anyone to comfort him since both his parents were busy fighting battles of their own.

That day when he came home, his parents were in town and planned a surprised birthday party inviting over some of his office colleagues.

As he entered the building, he could sense that there was some movement in his house, at first, he wanted to call the cops, however, thankfully he decided to check out himself. When he opened the door, he was welcomed with a loud cheer of SURPRISE!

Rahul was certainly not in the mood for this party as he reluctantly entered the room to accept greetings from everyone. He was especially not in the mood since his parents had also invited Kriti along with his marketing partner, who seemed all too busy dancing and eating together throughout the evening.

After an hour or so Rahul's dad who was searching for him, saw him standing on the balcony alone along with a glass of beer.

'You don't seem to be having fun, it's your birthday, after all, come on in son,' said Rahul's father.

'I am good dad, go ahead, enjoy yourself,' replied Rahul.

'You never seem happy with anything, your mom and I came down here, contacted all your friends, spend all the money in organizing this party and you haven't even spoken to us properly. What is your problem?' said Rahul's dad.

'Who asked you to do all this, half of the people you have invited do not even speak to me properly in office, you could have at least asked me before throwing this party' replied Rahul.

'Alright so now it's our mistake?' said Rahul's dad rather loudly for almost everyone to hear. Hearing the noise his mom walked in to join the discussion at the balcony.

'What's the matter with you two, it's your birthday today Rahul. We can discuss all these things tomorrow, but today at least let's cut your cake and have dinner together' said his mom.

'And pretend that everything is alright, pretend that we are a normal family. Mom in case you have not noticed my initials on the door does not read Rahul Mehra, it just reads Rahul' mentioned Rahul.

'Alright, that's it, I am out of here, please enjoy your birthday party, I would send the bill for your mom to pay,' claimed Rahul's dad.

'Happy birthday to the greatest son in this whole world' screamed Rahul's dad in front of everyone as he stormed out of the house.

Rahul kept looking at the sky from his balcony along with his beer, caring the least for the drama which was happening at his home. This was not the first time he had seen his dad overreact to a situation; he had grown up seeing these types of arguments happen every day.

The guests realizing the situation started leaving on their own with Kriti being the last one to leave hoping to at least wish Rahul a happy birthday, which she was too uncomfortable to say in front of her boyfriend. However, Rahul was in no mood to turn around as his mom too went to her room leaving the party hall empty.

Later that night as Rahul was cleaning up the room his phone rang, it was Nishant who was calling.

'Happy birthday brother, still celebrating with Bruno only,' said Nishant.

'Thanks, and yes,' replied Rahul looking at the empty room.

'Don't worry, I have the perfect birthday gift to cheer you up. I am planning a trip to the Himalayan resort along with Amar and you are coming,' explained Nishant.

Rahul who was too tired to argue knew it was an opportunity to be with his two best friends who genuinely cared for him.

'When do we leave? I need to arrange a temporary home for Bruno' asked Rahul as he finally smiled the first time that evening.

THE THIRD DIMENSION: EMOTIONS

Emotion simply means energy in motion.

Emotions are nothing but the feelings that we experience within us such as happiness, loneliness, anger, pride, anxiety, regret, shame, guilt, excitement, love, etc. depending on our experiences and the stimuli we receive from our surroundings and people around us. Every individual has a unique perception of the event and every individual feels it differently. That is the reason why some people are considered to be more emotional than others.

Our emotions are the primary influencing factor for every definitive action that we make as human beings. We experience emotions right from the time we are born. Gradually as we grow up, we tend to understand the world around us in a better way and also develop a better understanding of our own emotions.

Emotions are a key part of our life and they affect our overall being and behaviour. As humans, we are constantly experiencing different types of emotions be it anger, sadness, happiness, guilt, or anything else. The role of emotions dictates our actions more often than not. Hence, getting a complete hold of our emotions is very necessary to lead a stable life. The role of emotions in motivating behaviour is also an important aspect of understanding our addictions.

Also since we, human beings, are living in a close-knit society where our behaviour and action is determined by our past experiences, some of the emotions like fear, anger, love and grief are so strong that they force us to do things which one would not even think of doing otherwise. On the other hand, many people can boast about the fact that they have a good grip on their emotions, which has been the centrepiece behind their success.

There are many times when so many of us experience strong emotions. These strong and intense emotions are good but it is bad to let them overpower you. Most of us knowingly or unknowingly come into control of these intense emotions. In the situations like these our body secretes a lot of hormones which makes it difficult for our brain to take any decisions. During such times, our decisions become biased and we base them upon our past experiences. For example, when we are angry, we do not realize how our behaviour is hurting others and harming our bodies. In a psychological sense, this is a state where we have no control over emotions and thus our brain weakens in controlling emotions. There is a famous Buddha quote: 'Holding onto anger is like drinking poison and expecting the other person to die'.

However, people have their share of struggles when it comes to managing their emotions; picture this:

- Sometimes I feel that emotions are nothing more than a reaction to an event. Something bad happens, and I feel sad. Someone pushes me, and I get angry. Someone threatens me and I feel scared.
- I wish I was emotionally stronger than I am right now.
- My emotions imprison me, and I do know how to respond?
- The two of us are deeply in love and we find more joy or happiness when we are together. The moment we are separated we start feeling miserable.
- Being angry at everything comes naturally to me, how do you expect me to change after forty years of my life?
- Love, joy, empathy, gratitude, kindness, these are the kind of emotions I want people to remember me for, but I don't know where to start. Every time an event happens in my life, I immediately shift to emotions like anger, misery, frustration, fear.

Well, I repeat myself at the expense of being labelled a broken record, the answer to all of the above questions could be possibly accessed if we understand a little more about the word: Balance!

Let's keep going, shall we?

CHAPTER V

THE HUDDLE

The three friends walked out that evening to a nearby café for a cup of coffee. As Amar and Rahul were talking, they noticed Nishant being quiet and somewhat lost in his world.

'You are awfully quiet today my friend, all good?' asked Amar.

'Must be missing Isha,' added Rahul.

'Do you guys want to hear something interesting, promise you would not laugh or judge me?' said Nishant.

'We stopped doing that when we took up your friendship offer,' replied Amar as he looked at Rahul winking his eye.

'I have been thinking about a treasure hunt,' said Nishant.

'Is it being organized here by the café resort owners?' asked Rahul.

'No, a real treasure hunt,' said Nishant with a straight face.

'Really and I was thinking about going on a world tour with Lady Gaga, I wonder how many clothes I should carry?' said Amar as he high-fived Rahul.

'Come on you guys, I am serious here,' replied Nishant with an irritated voice.

'We are not in college and I don't have time for all this, come to the point,' added Amar.

'Yea, what's the back story?' said Rahul sounding excited like a small child as Amar gave him the stare.

'During my time at the ASI there was the treasure which I learned about; people call it as the Great Himalayan Treasure. It has also reference in some of the oldest history books. The treasure has its roots in the Gupta empire which flourished around 320 CE. During the time when the Gupta empire was on the decline after about 200 years, the legend says that the last of its rulers wanted to protect the treasure from the forces which were attacking their empire. Thus, they hid the treasure somewhere in the Himalayan region so that it becomes almost impossible to find,' explained Nishant.

'Where do you get to read, stuff like this?' asked Amar.

'This is my field of expertise Amar and all these things are not published in the modern books anywhere, you need to have access to some of the oldest libraries in India, and my case the National Library of India,' replied Nishant.

He continued to explain, 'In 2010, the Ministry of Culture, the owner of the library, decided to get the library building restored by the Archaeological Survey of India (ASI). While taking stock of the library building, the conservation engineers discovered a previously unknown room. The secret ground-floor room, about 1000 sq. ft. in size, seemed to have no opening of any kind.

The ASI archaeologists tried to search the first-floor area (that forms the ceiling of the room) for a trap door but found nothing. Since the building is of historical and cultural importance, ASI had decided to bore a hole through the wall instead of breaking it. There were speculations about the room being a punishment room used by Warren Hastings and other British officials or a place to store treasure.

In 2011, the researchers announced that the room was filled with mud, probably to stabilize the building. And interestingly, the ASI stopped publishing all information about the chamber from 2012 onwards. But more interestingly, when I was digging deep into this controversy by asking some of my contacts at the ASI, they said it was not all mud and rubble that they found. Apparently, they found some textbooks which gave reference to this treasure along with map,' concluded Nishant.

Nishant took out from the file he was holding an old piece of paper which looked somewhat torn, however, looking at the thickness and the weariness; the paper appeared to be quite old.

'My team found some remains that link the map during their archaeological expedition in Patna, the city was erstwhile known as Pataliputra, the capital city of the Gupta empire. The central location of the city of Pataliputra was ideal for the rulers to establish their administrative capital here. Pataliputra also acted as a base for the Gupta Empire to expand the territories of the empire around the capital.

It was also one of the important educational centres during the Gupta dynasty period. Pataliputra was also an important place as far as carrying out of trade and commerce activities of the Gupta empire were concerned. Interestingly, it is believed that Buddha, on his way from Rajgir to Vaishali, passed by this town and predicted that it was destined to become a great city,' explained Nishant.

'And you think that this whole treasure thing is for real?' asked Amar.

'I would like to believe so,' replied Nishant.

'I mean look at this map for once, there is no reference to any locations, all we can see are some alphabetical numbers and some drawings,' replied Amar as he passed the map to Rahul.

'Yea, I don't understand this either,' said Rahul as he passed the map back to Nishant.

'Of course, you won't, to understand this we would need to go back to the age of Aryabhata,' said Nishant sounding excited.

'Really and have you invented the time machine for us to go there,' said Amar sounding cheeky as he high-fived Rahul.

'Oh, come on guys, for once be serious about this stuff,' interjected Nishant as he waited for the two of them to be silent from their giggling.

'Aryabhata's birthplace was Asmaka but most of his work was stored at the Kusumapura region. In fact, Kusumapura became one of the two major mathematical centres of India, the other being Ujjain. Both are in the north but Kusumapura (assuming it to be close to Pataliputra) is on the Ganges and is the more northerly. Pataliputra, being the capital of the Gupta Empire at the time of Aryabhata, was the centre of a communications network that allowed learning from other parts of the world to reach it easily, and also allowed the mathematical and astronomical advances made by Aryabhata and his school to reach across India and also eventually into the Islamic world.

As to the texts written by Aryabhata only one has survived. The surviving text is Aryabhata's masterpiece the '*Aryabhatiya*'. Aryabhata uses the kuttaka method to solve problems that adopt the alphabetical counting system.

In today's world, two types of imaginary grid lines were thus used to define a position on the earth's surface: latitude, which specifies the north-south position and longitude, which specifies the east-west position. Longitudes run north to south from pole to pole, whereas latitudes run across. The crucial difference between the two is that while every longitude is a great circle, the only latitudinal great circle is the equator' explained Nishant as he stopped for a minute.

'In the seventh chapter of his seminal work *Aryabhatiya*, the value of the earth's diameter is given as 1,050 yojanas, which translates to 3,300 yojanas as the equatorial circumference which corresponds to a value of a Pi (3.146). The size of the yojana was, however, not fixed as it was pegged to the height of a man or the width of a finger. Therefore, different astronomers used different scales of measurement.

Modern estimates suggest that Aryabhata's computation was 39,968 km (24,835 miles), just off the currently accepted value of 40,074 km by an incredible 0.27%. All this may sound easy in theory, except when you realize that these remarkable calculations were made without the aid of an accurate timekeeping device (like a chronometer) or a standard unit of length.'

'He was a genius amongst geniuses, everyone knows,' replied Rahul.

'Exactly, also if you read some of the works of the Indian ancient mathematicians you would come to know that, Indian astronomers were quite familiar with the concept of longitude. They had the concept of deshantara – basically a correction for the local time at a longitude, calculated from the distance to a reference location, which was Ujjain. Since they could have determined the latitude easily using shadow lengths of a gnomon at noon, I guess that he used it to mark points on the earth at the equal latitude and measured the distance between them.'

Nishant continued to ramble for another two minutes without really caring to check if Amar or Rahul was following him. When he looked at them, they were staring at him with their eyes wide open.

Nishant understood their faces and continued, 'I know you guys are understanding very little from this, but the historical reference was necessary for you guys to understand that am not bluffing with this stuff'.

'Alright Mr genius, now could you please explain to us that what have you been able to deduce from this map?' retorted Amar.

'If my calculation is not wrong, based on these alphabetical equations, I could find out the exact latitude and longitude for this location, and then we would know where to start,' replied Nishant looking poised.

Nishant could see from their expressions that Amar and Rahul were still not convinced.

'Well look, there is enough evidence to suggest that this Himalayan treasure exists, the only way to find out is if we look for the first clue in this map. If we can decipher the location for the first hurdle, then surely, we may be onto something. However, if we find that the information is fake, we could just forget everything and go back home' explained Nishant.

'It could be fun Amar, remember the old college days where we would go onto the treasure hunt during our camping days,' added Rahul looking towards Amar who was still having second thoughts.

'Yes, but if this is for real then the scale and the complexity of this expedition would be completely different. Are we ready for this mentally and physically?' questioned Amar.

'How difficult could it be and with the three of us together, I am sure we can overcome any challenge that this expedition throws at us,' replied Nishant sounding excited.

'Alright if you say so Nishant, we are anyways on holiday for the next ten days, might as well as explore this so-called treasure of yours,' said Amar.

The other two friends nodded as they decided to take forward the discussion to their guest house.

***

'They are on their way professor,' said Raman sitting with Leena on a table not too far away from the three friends.

'Keep an eye on them and update me on the progress,' came the voice on the other side.

'Sure, would do,' replied Raman.

CHAPTER VI

FIRST HURDLE – THE CHANTING SAINT

The three friends looked at each other as they tried to decipher the map which had the clue to their first destination.

While sitting next to the fire on a full moon night, they could hear the howling's of wolves. Both Amar and Rahul could sense the discomfort for Nishant the moment he heard the wolf cry, they were closely observing his expressions as the noise would erupt from the mountains.

'What are you guys looking at, yes I am afraid. I am a scientist, not a hunter' said Nishant in an irritated tone.

'You do realize that the wolf may be standing in front of us during one of these treasure expeditions. What would you do then Mr Scientist?' asked Amar jokingly.

'He won't be able to run either, thanks to his Zomato expeditions,' joked Rahul as he threw a high five towards Amar from a distance.

'You guys should focus on the map, we have just ten days to reach to the treasure,' said Nishant as he stopped in between because of the wolf cry.

'Why did I join this treasure hunt, my practice was going great!' thought Nishant to himself as he gazed at the full moon.

'It's the full moonlight, they are howling at the moon, not towards you, you can relax,' claimed Amar as he giggled looking at Rahul.

The three friends went back to the map as they tried to decipher the first code.

'If I am not wrong this latitude and longitude correspond to the location of a temple within the vicinity of the forests,' remarked Nishant.

'And you expect us to travel through the entire hilly terrain and look for this temple within the jungle,' enquired Rahul.

'It mentions a picture of a saint as well, maybe somewhere in this temple itself, somebody who had been around for hundreds of years,' Nishant said.

'There have been many saints in India who have lived for more than four hundred or five hundred years, but this clue would have been much older than that, how could it signal about a saint?' asked Rahul.

'Well there have been saints that have passed on their legacy to their legions, maybe this could be a similar scenario for all we know,' replied Nishant.

The three of them prepared for their endeavour the next morning. It was an uneasy night especially for Nishant who could hear the wolves howling throughout the night. Nishant was up looking at the window as someone touched him from behind.

'Woooohh,' shouted Nishant in horror as almost fell off his bed as he saw both his friends standing behind him laughing out loud.

'Guys this is not funny,' said Nishant as he threw a pillow towards them.

'Get some sleep Mr Scientist and check your pants to make sure they are not wet,' said Amar as he and Rahul went out of the room laughing as they walked away.

***

Next Morning

'Alright, look, the driver would drop us near Shogi Hills and from there this place is close to about 8-10 km in the forest area. This place is not known to have any wild animals from what information I have gathered but we need to take all precautions,' explained Nishant.

'You guys would be safe with me, trust me, I have been on many forest expeditions with my friends at the training centre,' assured Amar.

As the three of them landed near the Shogi Hills, they were greeted with some pretty hard weather, however, they were determined to continue. On their way towards the forest, Amar took the lead and instructed his friends to follow him.

'Look, this is daytime so most of the wild animals would unlikely come out even if they are there, so we are safe. But do remember to keep your eyes and ears open all the time, anything you hear or see suspicious just tell me so I could run for the money,' said Amar.

The other two friends looked confused at Amar as he clarified, 'I am just kidding, just stick together no matter what, we would be fine.'

On their way to the temple, the three were discussing the origin of the treasure.

'Look guys all we know is that this treasure was hidden for it to be preserved by the Gupta rulers when their dynasty was coming to an end around the 7th century. They did not want any foreign rulers to lay their hands on this treasure,' explained Nishant.

The three of them stopped for a while to eat something from their backpacks as Nishant continued with his story. The place where they sat on the tree bark, the wood was still wet from the last night's rains. It was breezy weather and it was getting cold inside the forest as the three friends sat next to each other.

'Can I light up some woods, it's a cold afternoon,' asked Rahul.

'Yea but don't get too comfortable, we don't need any unwanted attention,' replied Amar as Rahul got some sticks together to light.

'You mentioned about the Gupta dynasty, how much do you know about them?' asked Rahul.

'I have done my research, though not much is known about the early days of this Gupta dynasty. The travel diaries and writings of Buddhist monks who frequented this part of the world are the most trustworthy sources of information we have about those days: 'The travelogues of Fa Hien.'

Chandragupta II, who was the last known Gupta

ruler, was a benevolent king, an able leader and a skilled administrator. By defeating the satrap of Saurashtra, he further expanded his kingdom to the coastline of the Arabian Sea. His courageous pursuits earned him the title of Vikramaditya. To rule the vast empire more efficiently, Chandragupta II founded his second capital in Ujjain.

He also took care to strengthen the navy. The seaports of Tamralipta and Sopara consequently became busy hubs of maritime trade. He was a great patron of art and culture too. Some of the greatest scholars of the day including the navaratna (nine gems) graced his court. Numerous charitable institutions, orphanages and hospitals benefitted from his generosity. Rest houses for travellers were set up by the roadside. The Gupta Empire reached its pinnacle during this time and unprecedented progress marked all areas of life.

However, after their emperor Skandagupta's death the dynasty became embroiled with domestic conflicts. The rulers lacked the capabilities of the earlier emperors to rule over such a large kingdom. This resulted in a decline in law and order. They were continuously plagued by the attacks of the Huns and other foreign powers. The Huns in fact came back to haunt the empire later and finally drew the curtains on this illustrious empire in the middle of the 6th century,' explained Nishant as he looked towards his friends who were surprisingly paying him attention.

'This was also the time when the Islamic empire was setting its foot in India. The Umayyad caliph in Damascus sent an expedition to Baluchistan and Sindh in 711 led by Muhammad bin Qasim. He captured Sindh and Multan.

Three hundred years after his death Sultan Mahmud of Ghazni, the ferocious leader, led a series of raids against Rajput kingdoms and rich Hindu temples and established a base in Punjab for future incursions. In 1024, the Sultan set out on his last famous expedition to the southern coast of Kathiawar along the Arabian Sea, where he sacked the city of Somnath and its renowned Hindu temple.

Later Muhammad Ghori invaded India in 1175 AD. After the conquest of Multan and Punjab, he advanced towards Delhi. The brave Rajput chiefs of northern India headed by Prithvi Raj Chauhan defeated him in the First Battle of Terrain in 1191 AD. After about a year, Muhammad Ghori came again to avenge his defeat. A furious battle was fought again in Terrain in 1192 AD. in which the Rajputs were defeated and Prithvi Raj Chauhan was captured and put to death. The Second Battle of Terrain, however, proved to be a decisive battle that laid the foundations of Muslim rule in northern India,' mentioned Nishant.

'Wow amazing, do you remember all of this by heart,' asked Amar.

'Look I am a student of history and an Archaeological scientist by profession. I get paid for knowing all of this,' replied Nishant.

'Still stuck on that scientist thing?' asked Amar jokingly but stopped in the middle since he knew it was a touchy topic for Nishant.

'But I am more interested in learning about Aryabhata and his work,' asked Rahul.

'Well, direct details of his work are known only from the *Aryabhatiya*. His disciple Bhaskara I call it

Ashmakatantra (or the treatise from the Ashmaka). He did not use the Brahmi numerals and continued the Sanskritic tradition from Vedic times of using letters of the alphabet to denote numbers, expressing quantities in a mnemonic form. He served as the head of an institution (kulapa) at Kusumapura and might have also been the head of the Nalanda University, explained Nishant.

'You meant, The Nalanda University,' added Rahul as he stopped Nishant in between.

'Yes indeed, in fact, it's said that a lot of his work was lost when that University was destroyed by the foreign invaders. Amongst the work that has prevailed is his magnificent work which is included in the *Aryabhatiya*. The most important work that I am using to find out the location of these places was included in the mathematical section. In fact the *Aryabhatiya* contains an introduction of 10 verses, followed by a section on mathematics with, as we just mentioned, 33 verses, then a section of 25 verses on the reckoning of time and planetary models, with the final section of 50 verses being on the sphere and eclipses. It's remarkable as to how much work was done during those times for which very little is known to this generation,' said Nishant with a sense of pride in his voice.

'Yea but I am thinking we must continue with our journey, we need to come back before dark,' suggested Rahul.

The three of them would have travelled for another three hours as Amar spoke up.

'Are you sure we are in the right direction?' enquired Amar.

'Yes, we are about to reach, according to my calculations,' replied Nishant.

'Guys, be quiet, can you hear something?' said Rahul.

The three of them went quiet and after a moment of silence, Rahul spoke, 'it's the noise of the temple bells, we are very near, it looks like it's coming from that direction.'

It was an old, mighty and symbolic temple. Even from a distance, they could observe its precise and harmonious geometry when viewed from all four sides and above, the square form and grid ground plans, soaring towers and elaborate decoration sculpture. To the eye, it looked old and architecturally picturesque.

The three friends were still admiring his magnificent grandeur as they did not notice a family of lions that was sitting right there in front of the temple. The three of them stood their panicking as they looked towards the entrance of the temple.

'Nishant you said this forest doesn't have any wild animals, how come we see those lions,' said Rahul with a tremble in his voice.

'I don't know Rahul why you don't go ask them, maybe they lost their way,' replied Nishant in a sarcastic note.

'Not a time to be funny,' reminded Amar to his friends.

'Did anyone ever had cold sweat before?' asked Nishant.

'Quiet you guys, we need to think what to do next,' mentioned Amar to his friends.

'What is there to think, we need to go back for now and come back again tomorrow hoping that they would have gone by then,' said Rahul.

'Let's wait and observe, maybe they would move away

in some time,' replied Amar as the three friends waited for a while.

'There are people inside that temple, I can see some movement,' said Nishant as he broke the silence.

'Yes, that noise of the bell is coming from inside the temple, so either these lions just came here, or there is some other gate to enter the temple,' added Rahul.

The three of them waited at the place for a couple of hours but the two lions seem to be circling around the entrance itself, almost as if protecting the temple from any intruders.

'Am I the only one who's getting the feeling that these lions are acting as guards to the temple or are you guys also getting that feeling?' enquired Nishant.

'Yes, am also beginning to have that strange feeling,' added Amar.

All of a sudden, the three friends saw an image emerging from behind the bushes on their right side. It was a tall man wearing a black robe along with a mask walking briskly towards the lions. The three friends were taken aback at the courage of the person who walked straight towards the three lions without hesitation in his step.

'What does he think he is doing?' asked Amar.

The man as he reached closer to the lions, stopped ten feet away from the lions were sitting. For a moment he looked at them and saw the lions looking at him too. Then suddenly with his folded hands, he keened down as if to pay homage to the temple in front of him. For the next five minutes, there was no movement, the lions still lying there were indifferent to the man who was kneeling ten feet away from them.

The three friends waited in horror expecting the lions to attack the man but instead, after a few more minutes the lions got up and made their way slowly towards the jungle. The temple's door was now open as that black figure made his way into the temple.

Nishant who was watching all this closely, finally spoke, 'shall we move in too, now that the lions have gone.'

'Well we don't know if they would come back,' replied Rahul who was still trying to search for lions fanatically in all directions.

'We have to take our chance, I would cover for you two and watch out for those lions, please make a run towards the temple gate,' said Amar.

'Come on hurry up, we don't have much time,' shouted Amar as he got into his position to look out for the lions.

Nishant and Rahul made a run towards the temple followed by Amar. When they entered the temple premises, they could not find that man with the black robe. They noticed that the temple belonged to Lord Shiva, with some of the devotees sitting near the Linga in deep meditation. On one side of the temple was an entrance that led them to the hall just behind the Linga.

There was an old saint who was chanting some words, as the three friends entered the small hall.

'Where are we supposed to go,' whispered Rahul to Nishant.

'Well, the clue is tied to the old saint in the temple. Let's just stay here and listen to what the saint has to say,' replied Nishant. The three friends sat there quietly listening to the entire sermon for the next hour.

'The old saint seems to be giving a very generic lecture with hardly any repeating words, what are we supposed to interpret,' asked Rahul.

'The map only references about the old saint,' clarified Nishant.

'So, what do we do with the sermon?' asked Amar as the three friends stepped out of the hall.

'Repeat to me those words which he was mentioning,' asked Nishant.

'All throughout his speech he was talking about the three pillars of living a meaningful life: Awareness, Belonging and Purpose. He also talked about attaining consciousness through various methods like awareness, concentration, chanting, visualization, etc. He concluded his talk by mentioning: 'It is only when we are suspended in mid-air, that we force our wings to unravel and alas begins our flight.'

'That's just strange, why would he finish on that sentence. It has absolutely no reference to what he was saying throughout his sermon,' explained Rahul.

'Maybe our clue is written here somewhere, maybe what the old saint is saying is the place where it has been written,' added Nishant as he moved to a corner to take out some thinking time for himself, and after a few moments, he suddenly shouted.

'Guys look around this side of the temple, you can see all pillars and we call know that this is the Shiva temple. If you would read the spiritual history, Shiva describes 112 ways to enter into the universal and transcendental state of consciousness.

'Maybe the old saint is referring to one of these 112 pillars!' claimed Nishant.

'Yes, but how do we know which pillar he is referring to?' asked Amar.

'The pillar could be hanging from the air just as the saint mentioned. This could be like the Veerabhadra temple of the South which is also a Shiva temple. Among the 70 stone pillars, there is one that hangs from the ceiling. The base of the pillar barely touches the ground and is possible to pass objects such as a thin sheet of paper or a piece of cloth from one side to the other. We need a cloth to check on each of the pillars, the pillar that would allow for the cloth to pass though it would be the one we are looking for,' explained Nishant.

'There is a total of 112 pillars in this temple, it would take forever,' claimed Rahul.

'Do you have anything else to do here, we have all night with us, it's already late evening, we cannot go back now' said Amar.

The three of them each picked up a direction as they started searching for the pillars.

After a few minutes, Amar shouted from one of the directions, 'Guys look likes I have found the pillar, come quickly.'

Nishant and Rahul hurried towards Amar as he showed them the trick. He took out his handkerchief and run it past the bottom of the pillar.

Nishant and Rahul were amazed as the handkerchief easily went below the pillar. It was indeed the flying pillar they had been looking at.

'I am wondering how this pillar is standing in the air,' asked Amar as he got up.

'It's the architecture; this temple is one of the oldest in the region. People here were saying it was built during the times of Ashoka the great! Look at the symmetry in these pillars, if you stand in a single line all of them seem to disappear, you could only see the first one,' explained Nishant.

'Amazing Nishant, when did you become an expert in temple expeditions?' asked Rahul.

'Well reading is all I have done to prepare for all my expeditions,' replied Nishant.

'Alright, what do we do with this pillar, it's impossible to read anything which is written on it especially during the night,' added Amar as he ran his torchlight on all sides of the pillar.

'We would have to wait for the morning sun. I am sure it would reveal to us something we do not know right now,' replied Nishant.

The three friends waited patiently as they sat in the corner trying to get some rest. Nishant couldn't sleep much as he decided to explore the temple.

He gazed at the dome on the sealing which laid in one of the corners; it had the sculptures of Indian Gods and Goddesses. In the middle of the dome was the Ashoka Chakra as seen on a number of edicts of Ashoka, most prominent among which is the Lion Capital of Ashoka. Indeed, it appeared to be a temple that was built during the time of Ashoka.

'What are you looking at?' asked a voice from Nishant's back.

'You scared me, Amar,' said Nishant who was taken aback.

He continued, 'Look at the sealing it has the Ashoka Chakra. When Gautama Buddha achieved enlightenment at Bodh Gaya, he came to Sarnath, on the outskirts of Varanasi. There, he found his five disciples Assaji, Mahānāman, Kondañña, Bhaddiya and Vappa, who had earlier abandoned him. He introduced his first teachings to them, thereby establishing the dharmachakra. This is the motive taken up by Ashoka and portrayed on top of his pillars as Ashoka Chakra.'

'I know for sure that the Mauryan Empire was the largest political entity that has existed in the Indian subcontinent, extending over 5 million square kilometres (1.9 million square miles) at its zenith under Ashoka. At its greatest extent, the empire stretched along the natural boundary of the Himalayas. The edicts of Ashoka, set in stone, are found throughout the subcontinent. Ranging from as far west as Afghanistan and as far south as Andhra (Nellore District), Ashoka's edicts state his policies and accomplishments,' Nishant took a breath as he gazed around.

'Having an edict here is something really strange, it shows maybe this territory is indeed unexplored for many years,' said Nishant looking at Amar.

'Well maybe we are in the middle of creating history here my friend,' said Amar.

Nishant had tears of ecstasy in his eyes as he looked around, Amar gave his friend a moment as he realized his friend needed some time to absorb this moment.

'The sunrise is about to happen, let's go,' Amar finally spoke.

Both Amar and Nishant headed towards the corner of the temple where Rahul was resting peacefully. They called out his name as the three of them headed towards the pillar.

As the first rays of sunlight hit the temple dome, the entire place glowed like shining jewels. Wrapped with the beautiful sunshine, the place spoke of splendid beauty, it was as if the Lord himself was shining around them.

'My favouritecolour is sunrise,' said Nishant with his mouth still open looking everywhere.

It was mesmerizing as the three of them looked at the pillar, the first rays showed up at the top of the pillar. All of them saw with eyes open as the letters revealed themselves in the golden light.

'Quick, click the picture,' said Nishant. Amar and Rahul took out their phones as they clicked the pictures for the beautiful sight.

'Well Greek indeed, I can understand absolutely nothing at all,' remarked Amar.

'Where would we go with these symbols I am wondering now, how we would decipher this'. asked Nishant.

'I know someone who can help us but let's go from here for now before those lions return back and turn us into their breakfast,' said Rahul.

CHAPTER VII

THE SECOND HURDLE – DEPTH OF THE OCEAN

Rahul looked at the phone as he moved around in the corridor waiting for the message. 'Still no luck with the first code?' asked Amar looking at his friend.

'Nope, I am waiting for a call from the translator,' replied Rahul.

Just then his phone rang; it was the translator who was calling.

'Any progress my friend?' asked Rahul.

'None whatsoever, this is not making any sense to me, they just appear to be random symbols, are you sure you captured the whole thing?' said the translator.

'Yea we are sure. Alright would call you back,' mentioned Rahul as he cut the phone.

'What happened?' asked Amar.

'The translator is saying he is not able to decipher the code,' replied Rahul.

'Should we go to someone else?' asked Amar.

'He is the best in the business, if he is not able to decipher this then I have my doubts that anyone else would be able to. Also, it's something we can't share with someone whom we cannot trust, we don't know who else is after that treasure,' replied Rahul.

'You are right, what do we do now?' said Amar.

Meanwhile Nishant walked in and the two explained to him the situation.

'Well we may be able to decipher all the three clues together, therefore we must pursue our journey towards the second clue. One thing is for sure that the clue was right, that means the treasure is for real, hope you guys trust me a lot more with this thing,'asked Nishant as the wolves howled in the background.

'Yea the wolves have answered for us,' replied Rahul as he giggled looking towards Amar.

'You were the one who was most terrified when you saw those lions,' replied Nishant jokingly.

'Oh I was terrified for you, if they ran towards us, you could neither run nor climb up the trees, you were going to become their dinner' added Rahul as he punched Nishant jokingly on his stomach.

The three of them moved back to their room to work on the next clue.

***

'So, you meant the next clue is tied to a tortoise who may be anywhere across the Indian Ocean, that doesn't make any sense,' said Rahul.

'Not anywhere in the Indian ocean, at a very specific location,' said Nishant.

'And that turtle or tortoise whatever he may be, would be standing there waiting for us with the clue in his hands,' mentioned Rahul as he giggled looking at Amar.

'On a serious note, we know that the India Ocean is the house for thousands of sea turtles or tortoises, how are we supposed to find the one we want,' asked Amar.

'I have a bigger question in my head; the average lifespan of a turtle is around 100 years, a tortoise maybe some more years. If the people of that era were to hide a clue, why would they tie up to an animal which may be dead in a few decades?' mentioned Nishant.

The three of them look confused as they looked at each other.

'Maybe we would find the clue to these questions once we go to the site at the Indian ocean. We should prepare to leave tomorrow morning itself for Bhubaneswar,' said Nishant.

'I am not really sure about this; we could be going in circles' said Amar.

'Look Amar we weren't sure about the treasure earlier but after the first clue we know that we may be onto something, there is no point turning back from here, we never know what lies ahead. We must at least go to Odisha to figure out,' replied Nishant.

'Agreed captain,' shouted Rahul as he winked at Amar who smiled while Nishant shook his head.

The three of them prepared for their flight the next morning to Bhubaneswar and from there towards the Rushikulya Beach, which is one of the largest inhabitants of the sea turtles in India.

***

'What a beautiful day,' said Rahul as he looked out of the self-driven car which they had hired.

'What a beautiful city,' added Nishant.

'Alright, enough of your beautiful lines, tell me something, there are about 250,000 Olive Ridley sea turtles that come every year to lay their eggs at the Rushikulya Beach. How are we supposed to zero down?' said Amar after doing some google search.

'A good question indeed,' said Rahul as he looked at Amar.

'The first thing which we need to do is to catch hold of some local guide who could familiarize us with the place as well as the breeding patterns of these turtles. I am sure there is something which we would find useful. Also, we would need to contact some local administration who could arrange for us a deep water dive,' said Nishant who was driving the car.

'Deep water dive?' asked Rahul.

'Yes, it's difficult to figure out if you would able to locate these turtles on the beach, they spend a large part of their time within the waters,' replied Nishant.

'I am not diving, you know am afraid of swimming,' mentioned Rahul.

Amar and Nishant could read the look on Rahul's face as they smiled at each other.

'You remember during the college Nishant, that pool party,' said Amar.

'Yes, how can I forget that day,' said Nishant looking at the rear mirror to see Rahul who was sitting on the backside of the car. Rahul seemed least interested in recollecting that incident.

'Guys, it's been fifteen years now, would you let go of that incident now,' said Rahul obviously disinterested to talk about the incident.

'My friend, it's difficult to forget, do you know where Ankita is now Amar,' asked Nishant.

'No, but I am sure Rahul is keeping track,' said Amar as the two friends laughed.

'Rahul tell me something did you actually accidentally fell in the swimming pool or you dived in the pool intentionally so that Ankita could lift you out?' asked Nishant.

'Of course, he dived intentionally, where else he would have got a chance, apart from that party. He had been after Ankita for long and she had not even paid proper attention,' replied Amar.

Rahul seemed least interested in continuing with the topic as he said, 'can we talk about our next clue and the way forward, instead of me and Ankita.'

Nishant smiled back at Amar as the two agreed to let go of the topic before Amar said, 'Where are we guys putting up?'

'I have booked some local three-star hotel in Bhubaneswar since I didn't want to make much noise about our adventures, we would go there directly, take some rest, and head towards the beach tomorrow morning' replied Nishant.

The three of them reached the hotel and were checking in at the reception, they could see some more people sitting around in the small reception area.

***

'Professor the three of them are here, we are also putting up in the same hotel and have asked the waiters to bug their rooms with a transmitter, we can hear all that they speak,' said Leena as she sat there next to Raman in the hotel reception.

'Great, keep an eye on them,' replied the voice from another side.

***

The three friends headed towards their room for some much-needed rest. Later that night as they were planning for their next day, Nishant looked for answers to the many questions which were circling around his head.

'I am still trying to understand as to how we would proceed with this one, guys any clue,' enquired Rahul.

'As always let's start with what we know so far about this turtle clue,' said Amar.

Alright, here's what I know, 'In Hindu mythology, the god Vishnu took the form of a turtle to carry the world on his back. The second time Vishnu was reborn (his second avatar) was as a half-man, half turtle. Vishnu was called Kurma during his second avatar. Most importantly it is often regarded as a symbol of good luck as well as prosperity. Am beginning to think all of that has some correlation to our journey,' explained Nishant.

'Well now you are an expert in Hindu Mythology,' said Amar.

'This is common knowledge, my friend, let's not give him too much credit' replied Rahul smiling at Amar.

'Are you sure the coordinates of this location tell us

that it's in the middle of the Bay of Bengal?' asked Rahul looking at Nishant who was standing near the study table with the map in front of him.

'Well if we found the first location of the clue right, it means that my calculations are correct. According to this map, the location is 4.5 nautical miles from the Rushikulya Beach,' explained Nishant still looking at the map as he circled the location.

Just then Rahul's phone rang and as he took out his phone, the ringtone was from the movie Titanic with Celine Deon singing, 'My heart will go on…'

'Sorry guys I need to take this,' said Rahul.

'Nice ringtone Jack. Is it Ankita calling?' mentioned Amar winking an eye towards Rahul just as was leaving the room.

Nishant was unmoved as Amar noticed him. 'Are you alright, did the ringtone reminded you of Isha,' jokingly asked Amar.

'Well that's it, there is our answer,' replied Nishant as he ran to pick up his phone. In front of Amar, Nishant typed the words Turtle Ship as he showed Amar the picture.

After doing some research he spoke: 'The Japanese invasions of Korea during the 15th century were extremely well prepared, enormous undertakings. Initially, the Japanese made great progress, defeating the Korean defenders at every encounter. Korean defenders had a decisive weapon of their own: The Turtle Ship! Developed and deployed by Korea's brilliant admiral, Yi Sun-sin, the Turtle Ship (known among the Koreans as Geobukseon) was a coastal defines galley,' explained Nishant reading from the search he did on his phone.

'The Guptas were also believed to have built their sea infantry consisting of ships. All this started under, Chandragupta II. By defeating the satrap of Saurashtra, he further expanded his kingdom to the coastline of the Bay of Bengal. Trade and commerce flourished both within the country and outside. Silk, cotton, spices, medicine, priceless gemstones, pearl, precious metal and steel were exported by sea. The seaports of Tamralipta and Sopara which is known as Nala Sopara now consequently became busy hubs of maritime trade. The five arms of the Gupta military included infantry, cavalry, chariot, elephants and ships. Gunaighar copper plate inscription of Vainyagupta mentions ships. In fact, ships had become an integral part of the Indian military in the 6th century AD.' explained Nishant.

Rahul meanwhile had entered back to the room and could hear the entire commentary.

'Now, given the architecture was so well developed under the Gupta empire, they may have also developed the so call Turtle ship and it's also possible that one of the remains of that ship is still lying within the Bay of Bengal' claimed Nishant with an excited voice.

Amar and Rahul were looking at each other with a glimmer of hope.

'Well there is only one way to find out, we would need to explore the sea at the particular location where you have highlighted in the map,' said Amar picking up the map.

'Amar, we know you are an expert swimmer who has also done sea diving, so we are relying on you for this task,' said Nishant looking towards Amar.

'Yea, but I am not going in there without you guys, we would go together,' replied Amar.

'Of course, we would accompany you,' said Rahul looking towards Nishant who wasn't sure.

'It's been years since I got into a swimming pool and you guys are expecting me to dive into the ocean, not sure how that would turn out to be,' said Nishant with a worried look.

'We need help from the local authorities, you cannot do deep-sea diving without informing the local coastguards,' claimed Amar.

***

'Informing the coastguard would open a can of worms, they would never be able to answer the questions that the local coastguard throws at them,' said Raman looking at Leena as the two of them listened to the conversation in the next room.

'Inform the professor, I would listen to their conversation,' instructed Leena.

Raman moved out to the other room as Leena started

overhearing the conversation in the next room. The three friends were still contemplating, not able to figure out the next steps.

After a few minutes, Raman stepped back into the room. 'The professor has said he would take care of the problem, he has asked to keep an eye on the three of them to ensure that they do not end up doing something stupid,' said Raman.

Leena nodded as she continued to overhear the conversation.

'They have decided to wait till the evening to figure out the next steps,' said Leena as she kept the headphone aside.

***

The professor was speaking from his phone sitting in the chamber while looking at the watch he was wearing on his left hand.

'You must make it feel like you are there to help them without really knowing about the treasure, I cannot risk them going to the local authorities. It's already 3 PM, make sure your person reaches them before 6 PM at any cost,' explained the professor.

The unknown voice on the other side just said yes as the conversation ended. The professor picked up the other mobile phone which he was carrying to dial Raman.

'Keep an eye on them till 6 PM, my person would reach there before that to take care of the problem,' instructed the professor.

'Yes, we would take care of that, Nishant did go down to the reception to enquire about any travel agents which offer sea diving services, I was there at the reception itself,' explained Raman.

'Great, now I know what to do, wait for my instructions' replied the professor as he put the phone down.

***

There was a knock on the door as the three friends were having their evening tea. When Amar got up to open, he saw a man wearing the traditional white kurta and dhoti with a gumcha on his shoulder.

'Namaskar, somebody enquired about a sea diving from your room, the person at the reception has send me here,' said that person who was standing in the room.

'Yes, we did enquire, please come in,' replied Amar.

Nishant and Rahul who overheard the conversation welcomed the man in the room. The man seated himself comfortably on the chair and smiled towards the three friends.

'Sir my name is Narayan, please tell me which beach you would like to visit for sea diving,' asked Narayan already knowing the answer.

'Please have some tea,' replied Rahul as he offered a cup to Narayan who accepted it gracefully.

'Mr Narayan, we are doing some research on the deep-sea creatures and marine life as well as the old ships which may have sunk in the past. I work at the Archaeological Survey of India and currently working on underwater archaeology,' explained Nishant as he showed to Narayan his card to gain his trust.

Both Amar and Rahul looked at each other appreciating Nishant for the clever hand he just played and then turning towards Narayan to hear his response. Narayan was too nodding his head as Nishant continued.

'We would like to explore if there are any shipwrecks in the Bay of Bengal region, I have heard a lot about them,' asked Nishant.

'Sir, well you have come to the right place then, we have had explorers like you come in the past as well,' claimed Narayan.

'So you know all about the shipwrecks that have happened in the region,' asked Rahul as Nishant got up to pick up the map.

'Narayan our findings suggest that this region in the Bay of Bengal is enriched with the marine life,' said Nishant showing the area that he had encircled on the map.

'Do we have any shipwrecks in this region, so we could do our research for both the marine life as well the shipwreck,' Nishant continued.

Amar and Nishant eagerly looked at Narayan as his confirmation would seal their claim about the turtle-shaped ship which may have sunk in this region.

'Sir, this area is famous for a very old ship, which had sunk many centuries ago, there is very little wreck which is available and also it's very deep down inside, therefore very few divers dare to explore that region,' replied Narayan.

'Can you arrange for the sea dive for us, we are not worried about the depth' asked Amar.

Rahul meanwhile tapped on Nishant's shoulders as there were visible signs of him feeling worried hearing about the depth of the shipwreck.

'Sir I am sure my team can arrange for the dive, though we have never explored this region either, however, I am confident we can get this done. When would you like to proceed?' asked Narayan.

'At the earliest possible, we can do tomorrow as well if your team could arrange,' replied Amar who seemed most excited amongst the group.

'Sure, let me check with my team and come back to you,' replied Narayan as he stepped out to make a call.

Narayan stepped out as he entered where Raman and Leena were sitting just around the corner.

'The approvals are already in place at the instructions of the professor, I am just buying out some time so that they get the feeling that I am speaking with my team,' said Narayan as he looked at Raman and Leena.

'The coast guard has given their go-ahead?' asked Leena.

'Yes, the professor knew that Nishant would likely play the underwater archaeology card, therefore the authorities have also been informed accordingly, we are all set for tomorrow,' claimed Narayan.

After a few minutes, he asked Raman to check if the bay is clear for him to go back to the room where the three friends were waiting for him. Narayan ringed the bell as Amar opened the door again.

'Sir, it's all been taken care of, we can proceed with the sea dive tomorrow. My team would take care of all the approvals,' said Narayan in a frenzied voice.

'That is great, thank you so much,' replied Amar.

'My driver would pick you up at 6 AM, we would need to do this early morning before that route opens up for other ships to move. I hope that is alright,' asked Narayan.

'Yes, absolutely we would be ready by 6 AM, just one more thing, would your team also dive with us since this involves deep-sea diving so were looking for some professional support' asked Rahul.

'Of course, sir, two of my divers would come along with you,' replied Narayan as he stepped out of the room after exchanging the usual greetings.

'This is so exciting, I cannot wait for tomorrow to come,' claimed Amar looking towards Rahul and Nishant.

'Of course, you would be excited, you are a trained underwater diver, God knows what would happen to me,' said Nishant visibly apprehensive.

'And you cannot ask for any training time either, you have claimed yourself as an expert in underwater archaeology,' added Rahul.

Nishant settled down after relaxing himself and then said, 'We need to plan for tomorrow since we cannot allow the divers to get near to the shipwreck when we search for our next clue. Let's pretend that there are two divers which come along, then Rahul you, and myself would need to take the divers along to another place within the waters. We can claim that we would do our research on marine life while Amar gets some time to explore the shipwreck himself if there is one.'

'That looks like a plan,' said Rahul nodding his head in agreement.

'I need to look like an underwater explorer, any tips you guys,' asked Nishant.

'Just don't start showing off your toned body to the marine animals,' replied Amar as he giggled at Rahul.

'Well except to the dolphins, they could mistake him for one of their own and add him in their group' added Rahul as Amar couldn't stop his laugh.

'Again, not funny guys, why am I butt of jokes in this entire expedition,' replied Nishant.

'Nope you are not, I am about to make a joke of myself with this deep-sea water diving tomorrow,' added Rahul looking visibly dreadful.

'We need to be properly rested for tomorrow's exploration, sea diving takes a lot of toll on your body,' claimed Amar.

'Yea but I think it's going to be a long night ahead,' added Nishant as Rahul agreed.

***

Next Morning

The three of them were ready as they received a phone call exactly at 6 AM from the reception that someone was waiting for them downstairs. The three of them headed down along with bags as the driver nodded at them and asked them to follow them to the car.

The drive from the hotel was picturesque as they headed towards the Rushikulya beach along with the backdrop of the orange sky. The rays of the morning sun were just beginning to peel through the clouds, and they could feel the cool breeze coming from the beach.

After half an hour drive the driver signalled to the three friends that they have reached and instructed them towards Narayan who was standing there near the boundary wall of the dock. Behind him were several boats which were parked in the dock. Narayan looked at them as he waved, he was still wearing the same traditional dress which he was wearing yesterday.

'Good morning sir,' said Narayan as he greeted the three friends as they came near to the dock.

'Good morning, you are not coming with us?' asked Nishant.

'No sir, my team would take it up from here, they are waiting for you, the small boat would take you to the main ship. Please come with me,' replied Narayan.

The three friends followed Narayan as he got into a small cabin cruiser that was parked at the end of the dock. The sailor started the cruiser as the breeze rubbed against the three friends. It wasn't long before the cruiser had covered its 4.5 nautical miles and the three friends observed a ship from far which was waiting for their arrival.

'Did you find it strange that this man never discussed the price he was going to charge from us?' asked Nishant to his two friends noticing that Narayan was seated far away.

'Maybe he would do now or perhaps it's culturally offensive to talk about money here before taking the services,' replied Amar in a hurry not wanting to distract himself from the exploration he is about to undertake.

'Yea, now that you have mentioned I find it surprising too,' added Rahul.

'If you guys could please discuss this later, we are about to start our exploration,' replied Amar in a thwart voice.

'To be honest, that's the part I am more worried about,' mentioned Nishant.

Narayan meanwhile signalled to the three friends that it was time to move as the cruiser neared the ship.

***

One Hour Earlier

'Where are they?' asked the professor.

'They are about to reach, I am waiting for them at the dock,' replied Narayan.

'Alright great, drop me a message once they have reached,' said the professor.

'Sure, what's your plan professor, do we take away the clue from them once they are done? If you want, we can drop them dead here at the sea itself, no one will even notice,' asked Narayan.

'No, you moron, we still need them to find the next clues which lead us to the treasure. Help them find the clue in whichever way you could without letting them know that you are aware of the treasure. I trust you can handle that,' instructed the professor in an authoritative voice.

'Sure Sir, no problem, one of the divers is Leena who mentioned she was an expert in sea diving' mentioned Narayan.

'I know, she is a GOAT, keep me posted,' replied the professor as he hung the phone.

***

Present Moment

The three friends moved out of the cruiser and got onto the big ship.

'I am pretty sure something is not right here, that is the same girl I saw at the reception when we were checking in,' mentioned Nishant to Rahul.

'Are you sure about that?' asked Rahul.

'Yes, I am sure but don't tell anything to Amar for now, he is too excited for the sea dive and not thinking straight at this stage,' replied Nishant.

'What do we do now?' asked Rahul.

'We are in the middle of the sea, what options do we have. We would have to proceed as planned but keep your eyes and ears open,' replied Nishant as he put on a fake smile towards the diver who came forward to dress him up with a diving suit.

'Hello, my name is Aarti and he is my fellow instructor Abheer. Does anyone of you have any experience in sea diving,' asked Leena.

'Yes, I have some experience but the two of them would need your help as they are doing after a long period,' replied Amar as he was wearing his diving suit.

'Alright great, Abheer here would dive along with you sir and I would tag along with you Rahul,' mentioned Leena looking towards Nishant.

Nishant looked towards Rahul trying to signal that how did she had come to know about your name, but Rahul could not grasp as he was happy to tag along with a beautiful girl.

'All the best guys, I would wait for you here at the ship,' announced Narayan as the five of them started moving down the ladder. Before that Aarti and Abheer had explained to them the hand signals to converse underwater and then announced:

'From what we know the shipwreck is about 9000 feet below this ship, that's a lot of distance to cover so let's take our good time. Let's stay together, especially you and Rahul please don't leave our hands as we move downwards,' announced Leena.

The sea was buzzing with its dormant strength with the waves crawling gently to the shore as the neon blue sky above created a mesmerizing setting. The turquoise water battered lightly against the five of them making it a seesaw as they pulled up the spandex suit and prepping up their oxygen support before taking a scrutinizing look at the depth of the sea. Finally, as they dived into the sea, the water was cold, freezing cold.

Looking through the crystal goggles, they could see the underwater sea as the morning sky. The sea underneath was indeed a paradise consisting of a large plethora of living organisms. As they lowered down, they could see some golden fish hidden behind the crimson red-stones seeking succour from predators. A sea turtle came from behind them as Amar got interested to check its whereabouts.

As they lowered further, the light was beginning to dim as the divers put on their emergency lights to see what lies ahead of them. From a distance, the divers noticed the shipwreck as they divided themselves as per the instructions.

The shipwreck was shrouded in mist. It licked at the rotting skeleton bringing moisture to the deepening crevices. It had been a fine cutter in its day, a sail of finest linen and a sleek prow to slice the ocean. Now it looked for all the world like a movie set, somewhere in the distance there should be the sound of hooves, swords, or an intellectual argument approaching along the sand. But this ship was quite forgotten in its demise, bit by bit it became a part of the waves that beat it so relentlessly.

Meanwhile, Nishant and Rahul were exploring the marine life just above the sea surface where Amar had gone. Rahul was pretending that he knew well of the marine life as he noticed and carefully touched the various flora and fauna which he saw below the sea life.

Amar circled the shipwreck looking disappointed at what was left. It was unlikely he thought that there may be anything that he is likely to find there simply because there was nothing left in that wreck. Just then he noticed a few turtles coming out from behind the shipwreck going into a small hole which led towards a bigger hole where he could see hundreds of turtles sleeping at the surface.

As he moved closer, he could see that right between those hundreds of turtles, there was a small chest lying there just big enough to fit into the pocketed bag which Amar was carrying. This was the deepest part of the sea that perhaps no one else touched for ages. Amar carefully got closer to the chest as the turtles which were sitting next to it moved away.

At a distance, Nishant had moved along with Abheer as they were exploring around. Suddenly both of them noticed a white shark moving towards them mysteriously coming out from nowhere. The great white shark had a large head, with cone-shaped snouts. Its body was shaped like a torpedo with the top half of the shark's skin was grey, and the bottom half was white. Abheer was too afraid and as an instinctive reaction, he left Nishant's hand to move towards the sea surface.

Nishant instantly knew that he was in trouble since he had little experience on how to deal with such creatures. It was a surreal moment as Nishant saw his death in the eyes of the shark which was heading straight towards him. It was a moment that froze him, he wanted to move to the surface, but it was as if his body was not listening to the instructions from his mind. Just as the shark was about ten feet away, Nishant closed his eyes fainted on the floor. In his last moments of awareness, he noticed a black figure who had stood between him and the shark holding the Trishul or trident.

The black figure as he noticed was neither wearing any diving suits nor carrying any oxygen cylinder. All he saw was the black robe that floated in water as the figure used his weapon to scare the shark away from Nishant.

Meanwhile, as Amar surfaced again, he noticed Rahul there along with Leena, but they could find no traces of Nishant or Abheer. After looking desperately for a few minutes, the three of them decided to head towards the ship above in the hope that Nishant may have gone back. When they reached the surface, they were could only find Abheer who was scared to death as he described their encounter with the Great White Shark.

The excitement of finding the next clue was overtaken by the fear of loss of the friend as Amar and Rahul looked at each other as well as looking brazenly at the sea trying to see if Nishant had somehow been lucky. Just as they had given up, they saw at one corner of the ship along the other side, they noticed Nishant's body floating tied up to the water tube.

'He is still breathing, get him up quickly,' shouted Amar as the four of them picked up Nishant's body taking him inside the ship.

Nishant and Amar were desperate as they frantically tried everything, from pushing his chest to giving him mouth respiration. Finally, their efforts seemed to pay dividend as Nishant got up coughing out the water from their mouth. Amar picked him and made him sit on the side of the ship with the two friends sitting beside him.

'Are you alright now?' asked Rahul as Nishant nodded in affirmation.

'What happened down there, weren't you attacked by the shark, then how did you land up here?' asked Amar.

'I have no idea, the last thing I remember was when that dreaded animal was moving towards me at great speed,' replied Nishant reluctant to speak about the black figure in front of Abheer, Narayan, and Aarti who looked at him from some distance away.

'Sorry sir I got scared seeing that creature,' shouted Abheer from a distance, hesitant to come too close to Nishant who nodded at him to signal that he had forgiven him.

'Amar at least tell me that all was worth it,' spoke Nishant softly as Amar nodded in affirmation giving a signal towards his pocketed bag with his right hand.

'And now tell me which one of you gave me mouth-to-mouth?' asked Nishant.

The two friends looked and pointed at each other, finally breaking into a hysterical laugh.

CHAPTER VIII

THE THIRD HURDLE – SHANGRILA, THE HIDDEN WATERFALLS

'See that guy did ask for money,' said Amar looking at Nishant as they reached back to the hotel.

'Yes, but how did that girl know Rahul's name?' asked Nishant.

'Maybe Narayan had told her our names, what is the big deal,' replied Amar.

'Forget it guys, am I the only one who cannot wait to see what is there in that chest,' replied Rahul as he signalled Amar to take out the chest from his pocket.

Rahul slowly opened the chest as the two friends looked at him in anticipation. In the chest was a small piece of paper which appeared to be of the same era as the map which the three friends were holding.

'What does it mention?' asked Amar as Nishant opened the paper.

'It has similar kinds of symbols as we saw on that pillar inside the temple,' replied Nishant.

'Give me the paper, I would click a picture and send

it to the translator. Maybe he could now correlate the two clues,' mentioned Rahul as clicked the picture.

The three friends decided to take some rest and sit during the evening to talk about their next clue. Nishant could hardly sleep as he recollected the encounter with the shark as well as the mystery person in the black robe who had saved his life.

***

'Do you remember that man in the black robe who visited the temple, I am pretty sure it was the same figure which I saw during my encounter today,' said Nishant as the three friends sat in their balcony having evening tea.

'It could be a coincidence as well,' replied Amar as Nishant still looked confused, however, finally decided to focus on the next clue.

'The next clue is signalling towards rainbow as well as a waterfall and my workings tell me that this place falls somewhere in Tibet,' declared Nishant.

'So now we are going to Tibet,' asked Rahul.

'Yes, looks like it,' replied Nishant as he asked his friends for some more time to do some research on the place they were about to visit.

Nishant fondly came back sometime later with his research which he had done on the subject and narrated the findings:

'This may well be the most ardent adventure that we are about to undertake,' declared Nishant as he looked at his two friends.

'Have you guys ever heard of Shangrila, the lost city?' asked Nishant.

'No, but something about your voice tells me that you are about to tell us about that,' mentioned Rahul.

'The place is fascinating with all its hidden mysteries, the mysteries of the hidden waterfalls,' said Nishant sounding like a small boy who was excited to see his new toy.

'And what is the back story?' asked Amar.

'Yea your favourite part Nishant,' added Rahul.

Nishant started explaining: 'In Tibetan culture, the Tsangpo gorge is a place of spiritual rebirth, and in this mist-laden air it seems that science and legend are fused. What is fascinating though is the Buddhist stories of a secret paradise in the area of Pemako. According to Buddhist legend/history the great tantric teacher Padmasambhava (Guru Rimpoche) magically sealed off an area around

Pemako where he hid secret treasure texts known as Terma, these can only be found at the right time by the (karmically) right person known as a Terton or treasure finder the places where these Terma are hidden are known as Beyuls or 'sacred hidden lands' or 'Powerplaces'.

'Wow, one more hidden treasure. It does sound like the place we are searching for,' replied Amar with a grin on his face looking towards Rahul who was fascinated by the story which Nishant was narrating.

Nishant noticed his expressions and continued: 'Padmasambhava had described Pemako to the Tibetans as a paradise that they could escape to in times of trouble and rumour has it that the entrance to this hidden paradise is behind a waterfall.'

'Given that you are describing this place as that of exploration, I suppose it would not be so easy to get there. Do you think it's even possible to get there? How much time would it require to explore?' asked Rahul.

'In my estimation, anywhere between four to five days. But we would need the support of the local travel guides and the villagers. We would have to gather a team of explorers as well as arrange for the necessary travel to Tibet,' replied Nishant.

'I am still confused, can you go back to your story and explain the region again,' asked Rahul.

'Let me give you some more geographical insights so you understand this better,' said Nishant as started giving the background.

'The Tsangpo River, the main source of the Brahmaputra, flows placidly, from west to east, across Tibet until it reaches the eastern end of the Himalayan range, and vanishes into a terrific gorge. The bottom of the gorge is 9680 feet above sea level, and the peaks that hem it in on each side rise to more than 21,000 feet. The river emerges from the mountains some 35 miles away and is then flowing south and west at an elevation of fewer than 2000 feet. There was, therefore, a chance that the gorge might conceal the most stupendous waterfall' explained Nishant as stopped for a moment to show his friends some of the pictures which he had gathered.

Rahul and Amar were mesmerized as they gauged over the pictures with Nishant narrating the story behind their existence. The three friends went about researching some more of the place they were about to visit.

***

'My travel agent has made all the arrangements, we fly tomorrow first thing in the morning to Kathmandu and then travel to Tibet from there,' declared Rahul.

'Great, though I am still wondering Nishant if this place is so fascinating why hasn't anyone made any expeditions there yet,' asked Amar.

'That's not true, in the early '90s an American called Ian Baker and an Iranian called Hamid Sardar who was both living in Kathmandu and were both heavily into Tibetan studies and could speak Tibetan, both decided they would go in search of these hidden lands and made several visits to the area over about five years. At this time the Chinese were also sending teams of researchers into the area to try and find the 'Hidden

Falls' and the area also caught the attention of several teams of kayakers and river rafters. Their travel notes and expedition pictures would be of great help to us,' explained Nishant.

'What about the team of explorers that would need to accompany us?' asked Amar.

'I asked some of my contacts at ASI to help us and they have assigned a team of explorers who would accompany us, they would meet us in Tibet itself,' claimed Nishant.

***

'Professor, they are leaving from here first thing tomorrow morning for Tibet, should we follow them' said Raman who was listening alongside Leena in the adjacent room.

'Let them go, I have something planned for them once they complete the final hurdle,' replied the professor.

'Copy that,' replied Raman.

***

The flight route from Kathmandu to Tibet was less exciting though filled with some beautiful picturesque hills as the three friends took a flight to Lhasa Gonggar International Airport in Tibet. They were greeted by the local travel agent who took them straight to their hotel.

Whatever equipment, clothes were needed by the friends were already arranged by the local travel guide as he gave instructions to the three friends explaining to them the toughness of the terrain which they were about to go on an expedition to.

'Be ready first thing tomorrow at 6 AM, we would start with our expedition,' declared the travel agent as he left the room.

'Why do all expeditions start at 6 AM? I cannot recollect the last time I got up late ever since this treasure hunt started' asked Nishant.

'It was your idea my friend, the treasure hunt,' added Amar.

The next morning the three friends started with their journey accompanied by a team of a local guide and two Sherpas.

Their first journey was to move along the Tsangpo River until it advanced up to the gorge.

'How long before we reach the gorge?' asked Nishant to one of the Sherpas as they began their journey.

'We would reach there in two days, we would camp at night near a village,' replied head Sherpa.

'Yea, and that is for them, means much more time for us,' added Rahul.

'When I am going away from this trip, Neha would surely be proud of me,' said Nishant.

'For discovering the treasure?' asked Amar.

'No, for losing my weight, that is equivalent to treasure hunt for her' replied Nishant with a smile on his face which faded away quickly as he looked at the treacherous climb ahead of him.

'This Himalayan region in which we were hiking is one of the wettest and most rugged in the world,' explained the head Sherpa to the friends.

'Those are not encouraging words,' whispered Nishant to Rahul.

The friends were all sweaty from the exertions of hiking and climbing, but they were at elevation, so they were advised to keep their winter jackets on. The small villages that they passed by and stayed were quite small maybe 100 people at the most. They're just perched precariously upon the mountainsides. People, there would look at them in wonderment at the knives and other hi-tech gear.

To add to the treacherous course the incessant monsoon rains created thundering rivers which flowed as boiling foam sandwiched between towering peaks. Therefore, the grinding geologic movement resulted in endless landslides, rockfalls, avalanches and earth fissuring.

Nishant was holding Amar's hand or assisted by the Sherpa during the entire course but his will was strong as he passed through all these obstacles.

'Is it still the thrill of losing weight which is still keeping you going?' asked Amar to Nishant as they stopped to take some rest in a village.

'No most certainly not, that was dead within the first hour. It's everything to do with this treasure, I am sure,' replied Nishant who was still huffing because of the steep climb. As they stopped at the house of the head of the village, which was a small but cosy place, his daughter brought in some tea for the guests.

'She gave you the look Rahul,' nudged Amar as he looked at the girl who was still looking at Rahul while passing out of the room.

'Too bad she doesn't know that he is engaged,' added Nishant.

'Engaged?' asked Rahul surprised.

'Yea to Bruno, right,' replied Nishant as he giggled towards Amar. After some rest, the group started their journey back, it was during the second day of the journey they came across a camp.

'What's that awful smell?' asked Rahul.

At a certain distance, they saw fleshless skeletons in rotting clothes.

'These are the remains of the Tibetan refugees on their fatal retreat,' said one of the Sherpas.

'The local village people believe in shedding the flesh of the humans to the vultures and other animals. They believe it's a form of sacrifice, it's known as sky burials.' The Sherpa explained as the three friends looked at each other in horror.

The route offered everything that the friends could think of, a wild, untamed brew of beauty, history, mystery and tragedy.

As they headed north into the hidden and uncharted 'Inner Gorge' region of the Great Bend of the Yarlung Tsangpo River, they knew that that entering a politically sensitive, highly disputed border area that demarcates Tibet from India.

But the Sherpas said that they were well aware of the region as they began their journey towards the uncharted sections of the Inner Gorge.

'This area which we are about to explore has been described as the heart of the world,' said Nishant sounding excited about the challenging yet magical journey that they were about to explore.

Since most of the route was less travelled one so

the Sherpa had already told them, that this would be a treacherous journey they would have undertaken.

'We have time on our hands, let's take one step at a time,' said Nishant who appeared a lot less excited than the other two friends.

The three friends had only climbed about 1000 feet as they met with the first major obstacle: The steep drop of about 10,000 vertical feet to the Yarlung Tsangpo river. They stood there at the top of the mountain as they looked at each other. The Sherpas had arranged the help of two local guides who were to guide them in this drop through the suspended rope ladder. They had made all the arrangements for the drop down to be as comfortable as possible, but it was only Rahul who had experience with any ladder climbing or dropping.

'It's not as bad as it looks,' said the head Sherpa as he tapped the shoulders of the three friends.

'There is a comfortable space to rest for a few minutes after every few feet or so and these climbers are experts in this field,' added the other Sherpa.

The three of them geared looking anxiously towards each other. The first climber started making his way down as he instructed the three friends to make sure they maintain a tight grip on the ladder as well as make use of the rocks to support their climb down. Rahul was the first amongst the three friends to move down holding to the drop-down ladder. Around his waist was a tight rope which was tied up to the rock on the top of the mountain, it would ensure that have something to hold if they lose grip of the ladder.

Nishant was the last one to move down as they slowly

made their way down to the river. From below they could hear the sound of water slight rain started to fall on their heads. The rain was making it very difficult for them to hold on to the grip.

Nishant and Amar who had little experience in this were finding it tough as they draped onto the ladder, often needing the support of the rope to balance themselves. They both seem frustrated and angry almost regretting the day when they chose to take up this treasure hunt. Their muscles were torn and the little pep talk that they got from the head Sherpa upstairs was beginning to wear off. The rest of the climb down was beginning to look much more strenuous and filled with obstacles.

Though the quality of the rock was solid, the rain was making the climb slippery as did the wind which was swirling the rope from one end to the other. Nishant attempted to look down as he was not feeling comfortable with the overall experience, even though he had a support of a climber who was moving along at his speed. Huge walls of water splashed intermittently twenty and thirty feet up onto the canyon walls.

'Do not look down,' shouted the climber to Nishant.

Finally, after five hours of a climb down after multiple stops along the way, the three friends made their way down to the bottom of the river. They requested the group to rest there for some time.

'Are you sure we want to go ahead?' Rahul asked him two friends who gave him that look.

'Just checking; have your snacks, but don't eat too much, next up we would be suspended in mid-air as move to the other side of the river,' said Rahul signalling towards the bridge as Nishant stopped midway while eating his snacks.

To get across the river they had to pull ourselves, hand-over-hand, across a suspended, 200-yard-long, single-cable bridge.

'This whole treasure hunt was your idea Nishant, if I die here you are the one answering my wife and son,' declared Amar as he looked at the bridge cable.

'Oh, I have bigger problems, Amar, I am doubtful that bridge would hold my weight,' added Nishant.

'You have lost some on your way, so it should be fine,' mentioned Rahul as Nishant gave him the look which said he was unimpressed.

'The Sherpa just informed me that two porters had plunged to their deaths in the violent river the year before when a similar cable collapsed,' Rahul came back with that horrific news.

'This is the worst time Rahul, if you say anything more, I will personally throw you away into that river,' shouted Amar as he made a small run towards Rahul who hid behind Nishant.

'Oh, don't hide behind me, I would accompany him to throw you,' added Nishant as too ran towards Rahul who quietly stood near to the Sherpas but was still giggling.

But the villagers on the west side of the river claimed they owned the cable and were not going to allow us passage because we had only hired porters from another village. After several hours of shouting and animated gesticulations, the dispute was finally settled near dusk.

The ensuing treacherous river crossing will long stand out as one of the most exciting and dangerous things the three friends would have done, but they somehow made it to the other side mostly with their eyes closed.

Once on the other side we then had to hike the 2,000 vertical feet in the dark up to the small village of which was named asGogden. The sky was pitch black and one false step on this exposed climb would have resulted in a distant free-fall to the churning river below.

They soon found out that their Sherpa friends were now out of their territory and could offer them no further advice on which way they should continue. Groping their way through the soup of swirling moisture, they suddenly saw a young man who was standing right there in front of them.

'Is he the head of this village?' Nishant asked as one of the Sherpas moved forward to converse with this man.

He was tall and stood proudly erect as two hungry dogs cowered at his feet. He was a lone hunter who ethereally appeared from within the shrouded landscape. After some discussion, it was learned that he knew of a secret passage down into the gorge and agreed to guide the team. He also told them about the famous rainbow waterfall when he conversed with the two Sherpas. The three friends were elated about hearing this.

'You must be godsend,' said Nishant as he tried to get near the hunter to kiss his hand but was too afraid of his two dogs.

'Follow me,' the hunter said in the local language as the Sherpas instructed the three friends to follow them.

After trekking for about forty minutes the track vanished into claustrophobic thickets of bamboo where the trees were close together, so close that there was only space for one man to pass through.

'You are sure about to get stuck here Nishant,' said Amar jokingly looking towards Nishant.

'Please would you stop making these lame jokes? We need to move towards the other side of this forest area and touching down on the village at the earliest,' replied Nishant.

'Are we going to go through these Bamboo trees?' asked Rahul towards Nishant who looked confused.

'We must hurry up, there is no time to waste, the weather can change any time at this place. Unless you want to be drenched in rain, I suggest you decide quickly,' declared the head Sherpa.

'There is nothing to decide, we are going,' replied Amar.

The hunter decided to take the first plunge followed by a Sherpa and then the three friends. Hacking their way through, they trudged uphill to passes covered in sweat and mud.

They finally managed to pull their way through as they noticed the Buddhist shrine near the hill where they would be resting for the night. The three friends were most relieved to see the shrine as they needed some much-needed rest because of their travel. While the hunter, as well as the Sherpas, were used to this travel, the three friends were certainly not and were completely exhausted.

'We still have about 4,000 feet of climbing ahead of us

tomorrow, before we reach anywhere close to the rainbow waterfall, that hunter just informed. He said he would be back tomorrow' said Nishant while the two friends were resting along with him.

'How would we know when we have reached the rainbow waterfall? This whole region like you mentioned is full of waterfalls,' asked Amar.

Before Nishant could even answer there was a voice which came from the door of the small room where the three friends were sitting.

'You would know when you reach there,' said that voice.

The three friends noticed a shadow at the doorway. The only thing they could notice was the black robe which was hurling in the air because of the wind that blew from behind.

'Who's that?' asked Nishant.

The shadow just stood there for a minute not answering as the three friends waited for what seemed like an eternity and just in a blink disappeared.

Amar and Nishant got up and ran towards the door but they couldn't find anyone there. They only saw the Sherpas sitting outside on the rocks doing their prayers. Nishant didn't bother to get up as he was stuck looking at the doorway. Amar and Rahul looked everywhere trying to find that shadow somewhere.

'Who the hell was that?' said Amar as he came back.

'I am just too tired to guess, let's just sleep,' mentioned Nishant.

The three friends slept well that night in the Buddhist

shrine room of a small house. In the morning they began their long, gruelling climb up and out of the west bank of the gigantic gorge.

It was a very hot day at the start, and they sweated profusely as they inched their way up. The hunter had already warned the travellers that the area is very steep, and people often get lost in the trail due to the constant landslides and torrential rains. There were trees for make shift bridges and handrails.

'We must stick together; the destination is not too far' he said in the native language.

When the three friends finally reached the top of the mountain stretch, they were exhausted from all the bushwhacking. They had managed to hike over slippery fallen logs, across bogs, and through a dense wet forest in the last two days. By this time the skies had completely darkened with clouds and the wind was howling through the trees. Blazing lightning and ear-splitting thunder were exploding all around them.

'These are not good signs, we must rest. The spirits don't want us to explore this region, at least not today' said the hunter in the local language as he looked down the hills only to sea mist.

'What does he mean that the spirits don't want us to explore the region, we have come so far,' said Amar looking at the head Sherpa.

'We would do as he says,' replied the head Sherpa looking towards Amar as he instructed the three friends to sit down to rest near the rocks which were lying there.

The three friends could see from that distance another

larger falls about a quarter of a mile downstream as Nishant took out the pictures that he has shown to his friends.

Nishant explained,' The falls that you see down there are the hidden falls of Dorje Phagmo. In the late '90s, Ian Baker (backed by the National Geographic) managed to reach these falls with a film crew, with the help of climbing gear Baker managed to scramble 1000s of feet down the gorge to a ledge above the falls from where he measured these falls to be a touch over a 100ft, however, one of his crew members mentioned that when they had stopped filming and finally managed to scramble right down to river level below the falls and mysteriously when he took readings from here the fall was exactly 108ft. The number as you know has a very important significance in both the Hindu as well as the Buddhist religion.

Baker was convinced that these falls were the portal to the 'hidden lands' as he named these falls 'The hidden falls of Dorje Phagmo,' concluded Nishant.

'This whole region is full of many such waterfalls which have been hidden for thousands of years,' replied the head Sherpa as folded his hands to bow down the sheer beauty of nature.

Suddenly it was as if the rain gods had listened to their prayers when the clouds moved away for the glaring sun to appear. Just across and above the waterfall they could see the most beautiful rainbow that they had ever seen.

'Wow, how stunning is that,' said Nishant with his eyes and mouth open hardly blinking.

'Looks like we are at the right place,' added Amar.

'Let's move,' the hunter instructed the group.

As they made their way across the waterfall following the hunter, the three friends were dancing with joy and gratefulness to the weather gods. The violent plunge of the great river, coupled with the constricted stone-walled throat of the canyon, created the hydrologic 'venturi' effect whereby the entire river appeared as though it were being shot out of a giant fire hose. The waterfall though was only about 30ft as they walked past it towards a cave that was hidden was almost centuries past. There was a very steep climb just behind the waterfall from which they could see that cave.

Standing in front of the small threshold, the cool, musty air from inside the chamber leaked out through the crack and pricked the visitors.

However, it was pitch dark as they entered taking small steps towards the opening. The hunter took out the long stick as he burnt the cloth to light up the cave. The three friends too took out their torches as they followed the hunter. They were hesitant to move quickly since the cave had been deserted for hundreds of years perhaps and they weren't sure what would lie ahead.

The cave's cold, damp climate was an abrupt contradiction to the warm, dry air they left behind outside. They wrinkled their nose against the musty smell permeating the air of this place. Inside, the cave was surprisingly spacious. The visitors were able to stretch both arms out to each side and not reach the rock walls that surround them. Several inches of space between their head and the ceiling allowed them to stand at full height, which was not the case though in other more cramped parts of this cave.

They would have travelled hardly for about 50ft when the opening in the cave converted into an atrium as the cave branched out into two tunnels. All of them looked at each other trying to gauge the situation and figure out which of the two tunnels they must take.

Suddenly they heard of a distant roar coming from the right tunnel which spooked the visitors.

'Was that the roar of the elephants?' whispered Nishant.

'I think so, though I am not sure,' replied Amar.

The hunter meanwhile signalled to the Sherpa asking everyone to follow him to the tunnel on the right from where the roar could be heard.

Nishant and Rahul were reluctant as they looked at each other but they knew they had little choice but to follow the hunter who was probably the most confidant person in the group at this time.

The tunnel soon opened up to a huge opening which was like a dome with a small water body on the right side of this dome-like structure. On the left-hand side, the visitors saw a family of elephants just sitting around not caring to look at the visitors who had just intruded on their privacy.

The huge dome-like room had walls around as they noticed water peeping through cracks. On the other side of the dome was another tunnel, however it was impossible to tell if an area bathed in shadow will lead to an opening or is simply a wall hidden by darkness.

'Guys I have a feeling we have arrived at the place,' said Rahul as looked around the dome trying to look for the clue.

'How are you sure about that?' asked Amar.

'Well I told you that I have a feeling; there is no logical answer to that feeling. We must search this place, maybe we would find out something,' replied Rahul.

Nishant instructed the Sherpas to look around and let him know if they find something unusual. The group searched for the dome for any possible clues for the next hour but without any real rewards. The three friends looked at each other and signed off in dejection.

'We must proceed, there is nothing here,' said Nishant.

Just as they were moving forward, they noticed the dome lighting up as the rays of the sun entered through a small opening on the top of the dome. The rays were falling on the small water body lighting up the entire room creating a mesmerizing scene.

The visitors looked at the rays as they created a small rainbow behind the water droplets. The scene came straight out of some fairy-tale as the three friends were feeling enchanted by what they were seeing.

Rahul made the first move as he hurried towards the rainbow and the water body which now glowing inside. The water had turned crystal green and they could see the bottom of the water.

Amar and Rahul were still amazed at the whole setting and it was Nishant who pointed out that he saw something strange in the water body.

'Look at those signs at the bottom of the water body, the one which is glowing like crystals,' pointed out Nishant.

'Those are signs, do you think it is what we are looking for?' asked Amar.

'Yes, they are similar to the other two clues which we have,' replied Rahul as he took out his high-resolution camera to click the picture of the signs.

The rays would have only lasted for about fifteen minutes as the dome started to become dark again. The visitors were now preparing to leave back through the tunnel from where they came as the hunter pointed out that the elephants are leaving in the other direction.

'We must follow,' the hunter suggested to the group and without looking for their confirmation started to follow the elephants.

All the group members had little but no choice as they followed the hunter into the tunnel. They could see that the tunnel was going upwards from where they could see some ray of light emerging.

Suddenly they emerged from that rocky womb into sunny rays. It was almost a feeling of being reborn. It was a jungle on the backdrop of the waterfall, something which almost no one in the group anticipated.

The Head Sherpa asked the hunter if he knew the way to the village from this place and the hunter seemed to suggest an affirmative as the three friends looked in relief.

***

The Next Day

The three friends had chosen to relax for the entire day still recovering from what had happened to them during the last few days of their journey.

They were sitting at the balcony having their morning breakfast as Nishant spoke up, 'Seeing the elephants as that cave was just very surprising and strange, isn't it.'

'It's hard to believe anything that has happened in the last few days, forget about just the elephants,' replied Amar as he looked towards the two friends.

'Did you hear anything back from the translator?' asked Nishant looking towards Rahul.

'Not yet but now that he has all the three clues maybe he should be able to decipher,' replied Rahul.

Just then the phone rang as Rahul picked up, it was the translator.

'Tell me you are calling with some good news,' mentioned Rahul as he put the phone on speaker.

'Yes and no,' came the reply from the other side.

'What do you mean?' asked Rahul.

'Look some of these translations do not make any sense. As you know that the primary written language for their times was Sanskrit. However, the Guptas also invented the Gupta script was descended from Brāhmī and gave rise to the other scripts during that time. The symbols, as well as the clues which you found, do not point out any specific set of words, they appear to be highlighting suggestive adjectives,' explained the translator.

'What are you trying to say?' asked Rahul.

'Pick up a sheet of paper and write this down,' said the

translator. Amar hurried back into the room and bought the notepad and the pen.

'The first clue which you found in the temple was suggestive of the words agile or graceful, the second clue in the ocean was suggestive of being kind or loving, the third one at the cave was suggesting you be involved or focussed,' mentioned the translator.

'Did you write that, or shall I repeat?' asked the translator as there was silence in the room after he spoke.

'Yes, we did, anything else which is useful to us,' asked Nishant.

'Nope, nothing much, sorry if I didn't come up with anything better but that was all I could gather from the clues,' said the translator as hung up.

There was silence in the balcony as the three friends looked at the notepad in which Amar had written the words for the clues.

'I cannot believe that we risked our lives for that,' mentioned Amar looking visibly frustrated at the turn of the events.

'This does not seem to be making any sense whatsoever, they appear to be more like commandments or values rather than real clues,' added Rahul as he picked up the notebook.

Nishant was silent as he continued to look towards the notebook, his friends chattered looking at each other, not noticing that the Nishant was not paying attention.

'What do we do now?' finally asked Amar looking towards Nishant.

'I was thinking, that how come we received similar kind of symbols at all the three places that does account for something, it cannot just be a coincidence,' explained Nishant.

'Maybe would get the answer when we get to the last place,' added Rahul.

'So, what's next, where does our final destination taking us?' asked Amar looking towards Nishant who was glaring at the map.

'There are no coordinates to the last destination,' said Nishant.

'What do you mean?' asked Amar.

Look, just the picture of the mountain with an OM symbol on that,' said Nishant as he showed the map to his two friends.

'So, are we going to the place where I am thinking we are going?' asked Amar sounding excited.

'Yes indeed, pack up your bags, we are going to the Mount Kailash!' announced Nishant in a resounding voice.

CHAPTER IX

KAILASH – JOURNEY TO THE DIVINE

The three friends stared at each other as they were still comprehending the final step, they had to undertake the journey towards Mount Kailash.

Mount Kailash's height is 6,656 metres above sea level. It is not the tallest mountain in Tibetan areas. However, no one has climbed to the Mount Kailash summit. The ancient legend claimed that only Milarepa, a Buddhist monk had peaked Mount Kailash.

'You know that are we going to the centre of the world,' said Nishant proudly.

'What do you mean?' asked Amar.

'Kailash Mountain is considered the axis of the universe, the centre of the world, the pillar of the world. It is the place where the earth connects with heaven,' mentioned Nishant.

Then he opened up his phone to show something, 'As you can see from Google Maps, the distance from Stonehenge in the UK to Mt. Kailash is 6,666 kilometres, which is also the distance from Kailash Range to the North

Pole. The distance from Mt. Kailash to the South Pole is 13,332 kilometres, which is exactly twice the distance to the North Pole or Stonehenge. All of this surely cannot be just a coincidence,' explained Nishant.

'You know that the hiking to the Mount Kailash has been banned by the Tibet government. How are we supposed to arrange for the permission?' asked Rahul.

'As of now we are just going to go for the pilgrimage of the Kailash Mountain, we would have to arrange for someone who knows the path to pilgrimage, someone who may be willing to help us' replied Nishant.

'How are we going to find that person?' asked Rahul.

'Well we have come so far, we must trust our instincts, I am sure the path will reveal itself' replied Nishant.

'But first, we must obtain the permission from the local office at the Tibet-India Pilgrim Reception Centre' added Nishant.

***

The three friends had made their way en route to the yatra with Nishant particularly excited since this was the last destination.

'This is a pilgrimage around Mount Kailash. How do we know where the treasure is?' asked Amar as the three friends were walking.

'We need to go closer to the Kailash perhaps' mentioned Rahul as the three friends stopped for a moment to strategize. Even after ten minutes though they were still struggling for any real answers.

'You must sit here and meditate for some time, all answers would come to you,' said that old sadhu who walked past them as the three friends were having a discussion.

'Does he know about the treasure hunt we are on? Who was that guy?' asked Amar.

'I don't know but it may be worthwhile trying,' mentioned Rahul.

'Do you believe in all these things?' asked Amar as he noticed that Nishant has already gone and sat at the foot of the rock on the grass meditating with his eyes closed. Rahul joined him as he did Amar reluctantly but eventually.

After ten minutes when Amar opened their eyes, Nishant wasn't there.

'Where is Nishant?' asked Amar as he shook Rahul.

Both the friends looked everywhere as they found Nishant standing at one of the foothills around 50ft away from where they were sitting. When Amar and Rahul came near him, they saw him staring at a mountain at a far distance.

'What happened to you, why did you come here?' asked Rahul.

'Do you guys know which mountain is that?' asked Nishant as he looked at his friends who shook their heads signalling No.

'That is the Om Parvat. We got the Kailash right expect that it's not Mount Kailash but rather Adi Kailash,' declared Nishant.

'What do you mean?' asked Amar.

'Om Parvat is known for its formation of Om which happens during the time of snowfall on that mountain, you can observe it when you get closer. It's also known as the Adi Kailash or the first Kailash' mentioned Nishant.

'Are you sure that's where the treasure is?' asked Amar.

'Well, the first mention of Om was in the Upanishads, more specifically the Mandukya Upanishad, which is a sacred Hindu text that focuses on the different theories of the Om meaning. These texts are associated with Vedanta, one of the six Hindu philosophies, and the etymological aspects of the Om meaning are thoroughly discussed in the oldest Vedantic texts. They regard the meaning of the Om symbol as inexhaustible, infinite language and knowledge, and the essence everything that exists and of life itself,' explained Nishant.

'Therefore, it is quite possible that the kings of those times already knew about the symbol and thus were able to identify it,' said Rahul.

'Exactly, in fact the Om Parvat has been described in the Puranas which were also believed to have been written around the 3rd-5th century when the Guptas were ruling the continent, why didn't I think about this earlier' added Nishant.

'Alright, so how do we make our journey to the Om Parvat?' asked Amar curiously.

'Let's go back to our base camp first, we would figure out from there,' replied Nishant.

'I am not going without finishing the Kailash Mansarovar Yatra, if you guys would like to leave, I won't stop, I would then see you back at the camp' declared Rahul.

Amar and Nishant looked back at Rahul who was ready with this camp luggage.

'Om Namah Shivaya,' the two of them repeated together as the three friends moved towards the Mansarovar lake to complete their pilgrimage.

***

At the Base Camp

'From what I have been able to research about the Om Parvat, it's only 17 km from here, though on a completely different route,' explained Nishant.

Then showing his tablet to his friends which had the picture of the Om Parvat he explained: 'This was discovered by a young guide of Kumaon Mandal Vikas Nigam (KMVN) Mr Vipin Chand Pandey when the Kailash Mansarovar Yatra began through this route. It is also said that nobody has been able to scale this mountain so far. Some people who made such an effort suffered adverse conditions. It is also stated that even helicopters cannot fly over this Holy mountain. Sometime back when somebody tried to fly a helicopter over this mountain, it came crashing down. Remains of the helicopter are still there in the valley.'

'Well we need to start our travel from Dharchula and ultimately reach Navidhang, the last 100 km of our travel in all foot my friends,' announced Amar researching the internet.

'Alright but I think from where we are, we don't need to go back to Dharchula. However, one of the local guides whom I spoke to mentioned that we need to go to the local army camp office to get approval first before we begin our journey towards the Om Parvat. Let us start first thing tomorrow morning' replied Nishant.

The next day the three friends made their way to the local office of the Indian Army which is located at Navidhang. As they stepped out of the office, they were greeted by three men who were wearing grey suits and black overcoats.

'Finally, you guys are here, we were waiting for you for so many days now,' announced a voice.

The three friends looked perplexed as if not able to comprehend if they are the ones being spoken to.

'Do we know each other?' asked Amar.

'Not yet but there is plenty of time for the introductions, for now, we would require you to come with us,' replied the voice as he stepped ahead, it was Raman.

Amar who was well built too wasn't about to give up on this as he thought this was some thieves who were trying to steal their stuff. As he approached Raman the two men behind him stepped up showing the guns they were carrying inside their overhead coats.

Amar stepped back as Nishant and Rahul looked shocked. It was getting dark in the evening and there was hardly anyone near the place where they were standing which was just walking distance from the army office. They knew that they had to give in to the demands of Raman as approaching anyone could lead to things getting out of hand.

'Come, our ride is just across the corner. Keep walking silently just ahead of us, any sudden moves and you know what would likely happen,' warned Raman as he gently nudged Amar.

'What about our car?' asked Nishant.

'Give me the keys,' replied Raman.

As Nishant passed the keys to Raman he threw the key towards another man who was just standing six feet away. Raman signalled him to get the car and follow them.

The three friends meanwhile got into the jeep with Raman driving and the other men guarding the three friends.

***

We Meet Again!

It would not have been more than 40 minutes when the jeep arrived near an old house which was situated on the side of the hills and surrounded by a fence from all of the sides. By the time they got out of the jeep, it was already dark, and the three friends were starting to worry.

Just like the traditional houses the house was built using stones, timbers, and mud in various forms, such as sun-dried mud bricks and rammed earth for plastering floors and roofs. Just as they entered the house, they found it looked quite spacious from outside and two floors in length.

The three friends stood in one corner as instructed.

'Look after them, I would be back,' Raman mentioned to the two men as he stepped out of the house to move to the upper floor.

After about fifteen minutes Raman walked in with Leena who sat alongside him in the chairs which were kept at the side of the room.

'Why are we here?' asked Amar in a stern but somewhat concerned voice.

'Welcome my guests, we meet again!' announced the Professor as he entered the room and got himself seated in the chair which was lying empty between Raman and Leena.

'Don't look so grumpy, you have been bought here on my instructions. And I am sure that you would not mind being a guest of your good old friend,' added the professor. For the next two minutes, there was silence in the room as the three friends looked towards the Professor and trying to identify the somewhat familiar face.

'Professor Puri, is that you?' Nishant was the first one to identify.

'Nishant, always the brightest one,' replied the professor thrilled to hear his student.

Then the professor looked at Raman and Leena to continue, 'we go a long way you see, when I taught in their university as a professor, they were my most talented students. Always the ones to win during our treasure hunts explorations during the college camps. Boy do I miss those wonderful days,' added the professor.

'I do not understand all of this the professor, what's happening?' asked Amar.

Even before the professor could reply, Nishant asked, 'So you are after the Himalayan Treasure too, that is what this is all about.'

'As I said the brightest one always!' announced the professor.

'Yes, and I also know that your people were perhaps following us throughout,' added Nishant.

'My child you still know too less, Raman should I enlighten them,' replied the professor, smiling sarcastically while looking towards Raman.

'Nishant do you happen to know anyone by the name of Professor Srikant from the ASI office,' asked the professor looking towards Nishant, with mischief in his eyes.

Rahul and Amar's eyes were now fixated on Nishant who looked perplexed on hearing the name of Professor Srikant, however, he sensed that his friends were expecting him to respond.

'Yes, he was my contact at the ASI office, he worked with the National Library project which I referred about when we first met,' replied Nishant looking towards his two friends.

'He is a very good friend you know Nishant, someone who would do anything for me,' smirked the professor.

'So, when you came to him enquiring him about all the mud and rubble that they found, he planted the treasure map just like I asked him,' added the professor.

There was a silence in the room as the three friends were still trying to absorb this information.

'Wait there is more, actually, I had been keeping a tap on all three of you, ever since you moved out of college. I knew someday I would need your help with the Great Himalayan Treasure. The invitation letter from the Himalayan resort that you received at your home Nishant was also sent by yours truly,' added the professor with a huge grin on his face.

'So is the treasure real or is that also a bunch of lies that you have been spreading,' asked Rahul with a frustrated voice.

'Oh, the treasure is real my friend, and is so is that map, you have already seen that in your adventures so far,' replied the professor.

The three friends look at each other still in disbelief at the turn of events.

'And now thanks to you I am closure to the treasure than I ever was in past 38 years,' announced the professor with a loud cheer.

'All three of you are going to rest here and tomorrow we shall begin our final journey towards the Om Parvat, you better sleep well because tomorrow is going to be a long day for all of us,' said the professor as he started making his way out of the room.

'Raman and Leena please take good care of my students, they are our guests,' added the professor as he moved to the upper rear of the house.

'What do we plan to do?' asked Rahul as the three friends slept together at the corner of the room.

'What choice do we have except to listen to that crooked professor. Oh, I cannot believe I thought of him as my mentor and guardian, what a perverted son of a gun,' replied Nishant with visible anger on his face.

'Let's try and get some sleep, there is no point discussing anything here, we don't know if they are listening,' added Amar.

CHAPTER X

THE FINAL DESTINATION

At the instructions of the professor, the three friends were ready early morning. They all stood up as the professor entered the room.

'Good morning my dear students, did you have good sleep. Did I come in your nightmares?' said the professor as he laughed on their faces.

'Look whatever you are trying to achieve through this plan, we still don't know where the exact location of the treasure is. The coordinates for this location are not mentioned on the map,' said Nishant with a somewhat stern yet irritated voice.

'So, what did you had in mind before my people got you here?' asked the professor.

'We were going to explore the region leading up to the Om Parvat. We know that the expeditions to the Parvat is not allowed so we don't know how we were going to progress,' replied Rahul.

'But now you have me, my friends, there is no region

that is restricted anymore,' declared the professor in a proud voice.

'Just tell me where you would like to go and my people would take you there,' added the professor as he instructed his people to get the jeeps ready.

The three friends were asked to follow as the professor stepped into the jeep with his two men sitting with the three friends. Raman and Leena were following them on another jeep along with another gunman.

The jeeps took a turn towards the foothills of Navidhang which was hardly a drive of 4 km. After that, they were to track their way to the Om Parvat with a total distance of 9 km.

'Just remember it's a long journey and in between this time, I would need your cooperation. You know me very well, I do not like any funny business' added the professor as the three friends got out of the jeep to start their trekking.

The trekking towards the Om Parvat was steep passing through small villages. Each of the gunmen was tagged to the three friends while Raman, Leena, and the professor followed them.

'We need to slow down, I am not as fit as I used to be, let's take a break' said the professor as they had trekked for almost three hours.

The three friends sat down as they recollected their thoughts on the sequence of events. Rahul was sweating for most of the journey even though the temperatures were close to 2 degrees centigrade.

'Are you alright?' Amar asked as he looked towards Rahul.

'What do you think, we are being kidnapped here and being held against our wishes, with three gunmen after our lives. Hell, no I am not alright,' replied Rahul in a frustrated and agitated voice.

'I can understand what you are going through, but we are in this together. As long as we don't panic, I am sure we can find a way out of this situation' said Amar as he stepped closer to Rahul to console his friend.

'Any new plans in your mind my students?' shouted the professor who was sitting at some distance away from the three friends.

'Not yet but we are working on it,' replied Nishant.

'I hope your planning is focussed on the treasure hunt and not on how to get away from this situation,' added the professor with a grin on his face signalling towards the gunmen.

After some time, the group began their journey ahead as the weather suddenly turned cloudy.

'Looks like it's going to rain professor,' said Raman looking towards the sky.

'Yes, but we must not slow down, we only have today's day and we are still some far away from our destination,' replied the professor.

'Did you guys noticed something strange at all the three places where got our clues?' remarked Nishant as both his friends turned towards him while trekking.

'What was it?' asked Amar.

'Do you want to guess?' replied Nishant.

'I am not in the mood of playing games,' added Rahul still sweating from his head.

'Look, in all the three places we went there were some of the other animals near the clues,' replied Nishant as the three friends stopped to contemplate.

'Well it could be a coincidence as well,' said Amar.

'Well if there is one thing that I have learned in a treasure hunt then that is that there are no coincidences,' replied Nishant.

The group stopped as Nishant signalled towards the professor.

'I need a pen and paper,' said Nishant to the professor who further signalled towards Leena.

The group surrounded Nishant as he started drawing something on paper.

'Look, the first place we went where we found our clue, we met the lion, the second place which was beneath the sea we found a tortoise and the third place we found elephants. It could surely not be a coincidence,' explained Nishant looking at all the group members.

'What about the clues show it to me,' demanded the professor.

Amar took out his camera and showed the three photographs of the clues.

'This language is difficult to understand, which language is this?' said the professor.

'The translator came back with his interpretations, but it made little sense. The first clue which you found in the temple was suggestive of the words agile or graceful, the second clue in the ocean was suggestive of being kind or loving, the third one at the cave was suggesting you be involved or focussed,' explained Nishant.

'Are you sure there is not anything that you are hiding from us?' asked the professor in a stern voice.

'We are sure, you can speak to the translator yourself,' replied Rahul.

'Alright let's keep moving forward until we find anything useful, we are close enough to the Om Parvat,' declared the professor.

The group slowly moved forward except for Nishant who seemed lost in his thoughts.

'Come on let's move,' one of the gunmen shuddered Nishant on his shoulders.

'Whenever you are lost like this there is another clue coming,' said Amar silently to Nishant.

'Not sure but something is bothering me that I did not speak earlier. If you guys remember there was one more thing that was common in all of our three clues, the man with the black robe. He is still a mystery but if you noticed he somehow helped us at all the three places,' said Nishant in a soft voice so that the other people could not hear.

'It's all too much to absorb at this stage for me,' replied Rahul as he looked at Nishant who stopped suddenly.

'Snakes, the answer we are looking for is snakes,' declared Nishant without even letting Rahul complete his sentence. He asked the group to gather again so he could explain.

'Look, there are two things which we know. One is the animals which we found at each of the three stages and the second is the clues. The first animal we found was the lion and the first clue was suggestive of the words agile or graceful. The second animal, the tortoise, and the second clue being kind or loving. The third animal was the elephant and the third clue was involved or focussed,' Nishant stopped for a second hardly able to notice his excitement.

'Now there are qualities that we associate with each of these animals themselves. Lions we know are strong and agile, turtles have been known to be kind and loving creatures, at the same time elephants have been known to be involved or focussed. Somehow these are associated with our life in general though I am not sure how. Being strong is indicative of our body, being kind or loving is associated with our emotions, and being involved is focussed on, our minds,' said Nishant but before he could complete professor intervened.

'The only dimension which is left is the spiritual dimension and the animal which is closest to that value is the snake,' said the professor with a sense of excitement in his voice.

'I knew you guys were the right investment,' added the professor taping Nishant on his shoulders.

'We are close to the local village. Check from the villagers if there is any place which is famous for snakes,' instructed the professor as he looked at Raman and Leena. The group rested there, near the local shaft as the two-headed out towards the village.

'Oh, I have waited for this day for so long,' said the professor as he looked at the skies hardly able to contain his excitement.

It would have been about forty-five minutes later when Leena and Raman came back.

'Professor there is a small temple nearby which is famous because of its snakes. The temple is inside a cave. We need to trek two kilometres downside to see but it's a difficult trek, the villagers said,' explained Raman to the group.

'But I am sure it's worth it,' said the professor excitedly as he instructed the group to move towards that old trek.

The next two kms were tricky as the group tracked through the mountain tracks, it appeared very few people had come along this way. The last 500 metres were a straight 20 feet drop as the group came across a breathtaking view of the mountains across the valley.

'Great, another descend of the cliff, looks like we are getting used to it. If only I knew what I was getting into before I came here, I would have at least done some stretches at my home,' said Nishant.

'Hurry up guys we don't have much time,' declared Raman as he and Leena were the first ones to make the descend to hilltop. The whole area was covered with huge pine and cottonwood trees, but the small temple was somewhat visible from the hilltop as the group started descending one by one towards the slope that led to the old temple.

As they approached the temple, they could see that it had a descended look with plants growing from all of the sides falling over the door of the temple.

'Stop everyone,' said the professor as he saw the black cobra make his way in front of the door and suddenly disappearing into the woods.

'We have to be prepared since we would find many

more as we enter inside the temple,' declared the professor as he instructed one of his gunmen to enter the temple first.

The gunmen entered the Shiva temple as the group followed. It was still early evening, so the light entered the temple as he opened the door. It was a small temple with no visible signs of anyone inside. On the right corner of the temple was a small cave through which you could see the Linga which was surrounded by two or three snakes that circled around.

'Where do we go from here?' asked Raman.

'Shhhh, we don't want their unwarranted attention,' replied the professor as he signalled towards the snakes.

One of the gunmen called the professor towards the corner and suggested that there is a way behind the wall leading to some stairs. As the group made their way down the stairs carefully putting each step ahead of one, there was a sudden noise of the door closing from their behind. It was like all the wind had been sucked from the temple and it became completely dark inside.

'Somebody go upstairs and check on that,' said the professor as Raman signalled one of his gunmen. As the group waited there, the gunmen didn't return even after ten minutes.

'Where is that idiot, Ahhhhh. Come on let's keep moving forward,' said the professor.

The group would have climbed down about 200 stairs which seemed like forever since it was pitch dark. They could only hear the hisses of some snakes perhaps which made them terrified and agitated.

The journey downstairs opened up to a larger space

which was all surrounded by grey wet rocks. Space though had some sunlight which was coming from the corner, as the group turned off their torch lights.

'Have we reached a dead-end?' asked the professor as suddenly they heard the voice of someone from upstairs. The professor signalled to the second gunman as he hurried up the stairs to check. After some time, it was the turn of the third gunman who too never returned. Now it was Raman, Leena, and the professor who were left there along with the three friends.

'Shall we go back professor, I do not have a good feeling about this whole thing,' said Leena as she looked around the stairs to see if she could see some movement.

'We have come so far; this is a point of no return. Let's keep searching,' replied the professor.

'Look on that far corner, it looks some kind of an opening,' said Raman signalling towards that corner.

As the group started to move towards the opening, suddenly from one side of the rocks two cobras came and sat right in front of the opening, directly facing the group. These were large cobras that had their head high and made a hissing noise.

The group members suddenly stopped and almost froze as the cobras were merely six feet away. After a gap of two minutes which looked much longer the professor was the first one to speak.

'Nishant according to your idea, this surely must be the way to the treasure. The snakes are somehow protecting the treasure,' said the professor.

'But there must be a way to get past them, should we

fire at them' said Raman while trying to take out his gun.

'Don't fire at them,' replied Nishant.

'That's right Raman, fire at these three jokers,' said the professor.

'Don't look so surprised, do you think that we would have left you alive after we got the treasure. Now move and get these cobras away from our path,' added the professor as he asked Raman to point the gun towards the three friends. By then Leena too had taken out her gun as she pointed towards the three friends.

The three of them were bewildered as one side were these snakes who were hissing at them and on the other side the guns pointing straight at their heads.

'The snakes won't budge; they are the protectors of the Great Treasure' said a heavy voice that came echoing around the space.

Even before Raman and Leena could react, there stood two men right behind them in black robes who held their hands so that the guns fell off as the two men kicked the guns away with their feet.

'What's happening here, who the hell you two are,' the professor shouted as he started to make a move to help Raman and Leena. But before he could move, there was another black figure which came out from the dark.

The man who was wearing a black robe walked past the three friends who stood in the corner and the professor as he went closer to the cobras. Without even a hint of hesitation, he picked up the two cobras who formed a circle around his two arms to show their affection for their master.

The master was wearing a black mask along with cloth tied around his head so that only his eyes were visible. And those were some steamy eyes that shined in the dark. As the man with the robe signalled the two other men, they took Raman and Leena upstairs while holding their hands from behind.

'Where are you taking them and who are you people?' shouted the professor who looked both frightened and angry.

The man with a black robe suddenly came close to the professor as the cobra once again picked up his hood and hissed towards the professor, this time from a much closer distance. The professor stepped away in a hesitant reaction and fell to the ground.

'Our ancestors have been protecting this treasure for thousands of years, ensuring that it does fall into the hands of people like you,' said the man in the black robe in a voice that commanded respect. As he was about to finish, one of the other men in the robe came downstairs standing in the corner as if waiting for instructions.

'You were the people that broke into my house as well as took the map from Raman's car,' said the professor searching for the gun which was lying some feet away. Before he could make his move, the man who stood in the corner came close to the professor and held him from behind.

'Please at least let me see the treasure, I have spent my whole life waiting for this day,' requested the professor.

The man with the cobras in his hand signalled to his person as he took away the professor who kept shouting, demanding to be released.

The three friends stood almost frozen in disbelief at the turn of events as they looked at this man who was gently playing with the two cobras.

'It was you only who had helped us earlier and you even saved my life, right?' asked Nishant.

'I would answer all your questions, but don't you want to see what lies behind that door first,' replied the masked man as he looked towards the three friends.

'You mean the treasure that is behind that door?' asked Amar.

The masked man did not say anything as Amar gave a confused look towards his friends.

'You mentioned that you were the protectors for the treasure, then why would you want us to have that treasure,' asked Nishant.

'The treasure was protected so that it could be brought back to the people by someone truly deserving, someone noble in his intentions who would like to do good for everyone,' replied the masked man.

'Your destination awaits you, though you must solve the last puzzle' added the masked man as he instructed the three friends to proceed. Before he went, he stood there for a second and took off his mask and the cloth he was wearing on his head.

Stood there in front of the three friends was an old man with grey and white hair which was long but relatively less from the centre. He was having a small beard which gave him a look of an old master. When the three friends directly looked into his eyes, they sensed a certain kind of connection as they folded their hands, enthralled by his presence. Those were the eyes of an enlightened being.

'I shall be waiting for you upstairs,' said the master as he disappeared in the dark.

The three friends looked at each other surprised at the way all three of them reacted to that old man.

'Let's go, we have the one last huddle to cross,' reminded Nishant to the group.

The three friends reached the door and were trying to search for the lever or a handle that would open the door for them.

'What do we do, there is no lever here?' asked Amar.

Suddenly Nishant noticed the old stone on the corner of the foot of this door which was different in colour than all the other stones. As he cleared the mud which appeared on the white gem-coloured stone, he could see the figures of animals that surrounded the middle stone which appeared like a 'Yantra'. The yantra was represented by the four doorways which surrounded each of its sides.

'Wow, how beautiful is this,' said Rahul as he looked at what Nishant had just explored.

'Maybe I am right, maybe it's a yantra which is signalling the four dimensions,' explained Nishant.

'How do we open this door friends?' said Amar who was meanwhile trying to push open the door.

'The answer should lie in this yantra. Look at all the animals which are surrounding this yantra,' said Nishant as he placed his hands on the small stones which had these animal figures. When he was touching these noticed that they moved.

'These stones are mobile, they can move' said Nishant

with a visible excitement on his face.

'Do these stones have all the four animals which we talked about while coming to this place?' asked Rahul.

'Yes, indeed all of them and more,' replied Nishant.

'Alright, this could work, try placing the four animal stones right next to each of the four openings of the yantra,' remarked Rahul hardly able to control his excitement.

Nishant just did as he was told. Just as he placed the last stone in front of the yantra, there was a loud noise as the door move back to allow for some space to enter.

'It has worked, we are in,' shouted Amar as he put on his torch to enter the room.

As they entered this huge room which was well lit with shades of lights coming from a distance, they could see huge piles of books and literature kept in a corner. While on the other side were stacks of old coins which belonged to another century.

The three friends were stunned at they looked at each of these stacks carefully.

'These look like they are volumes of work which belonged to the Golden Era of India. Some great pieces of art, pieces of literature, scientific papers,' shouted Nishant as the three friends explored the entire room.

'These coins would still be worth a lot of money, right?' asked Amar looking at the bag of coins which were kept in a corner.

'You still don't understand my friend. The Kings of those times were not concerned about these gold coins going into the hand of their enemies. They were concerned about the real wealth which is all these great repositories of knowledge that would never find their rightful place. They knew that their enemies would never value this craft and would be hell bend in destroying this forever, just like the Nalanda University which was destroyed again and again,' explained Nishant.

'So, what does this mean?' again asked Amar.

'Do you know how much this could help establish the credibility of our great scientists, gurus, story writers, musicians, and literature writers of those times,' explained Nishant who had tears in his eyes seeing the treasure in front of him.

'The discovery of this nature is the culmination of

thousands of years waiting and it deserves to be used for the right purpose, for the betterment of humanity,' added Rahul.

'A treasure worth its wait my friends,' shouted Nishant as the three friends came together to hug each other at their remarkable exploration.

FINAL CHAPTER

BALANCE COMES FROM WITHIN!

The old master was quiet as the three friends sat there on the rocks waiting for him to say his first words.

The treasure is worth its find master, said Nishant.

The master smiled for a moment and then added: That is true but the treasure within us is more precious than any treasure you would find on this planet. The problem is that most people are looking for the treasure in the wrong place.

Why do you say so, asked Rahul?

We are the most knowledgeable creature on this planet, the mind that we have today has come to this place after millions of years of evolution. Just look around you, the kind of world we have created for ourselves, the advancements in technology, our life is more comfortable than ever.

The generations before us had to deal with so many challenges primarily concerning pandemics, diseases, and wars. But we have been able to overcome most of these challenges coming into the 21st Century. Yes, we had the scare of the COVID-19, millions of people still die due to AIDS across the globe and of course, the war threats are still rampant in some countries like Syria, Iraq, and the Middle East. But 100 years ago, these were challenges that affected almost everyone's life, today a large part of the population is free from these challenges which were a threat to their lives. Thus, their survival is mostly taken care of, it's been organized in a manner that was never organized.

Yet, when you go around asking people if they are truly happy and joyous in their lives, the answer would be likely a No! That's because we have not paid attention to the way this human life works. The amount of time and efforts that are being spent exploring the mysteries of this universe should also find its way into exploring the way this life works. And the best part of exploring human life is that it does not require anyone to spend millions of dollars designing complicated machines that go into space or perform complicated scientific experiments on the human brain. All it requires is for us to pay a little attention, the kind of attention that this human mechanism which is the most complicated machine on this planet deserves. I am not someone who is against scientific experimentation; in fact, thanks to our scientists we know more about our human mind than we knew at any point in the past.

All the money, the valuables, in fact the entire economic model is the manifestation of the human mind. Everything that happened on this planet first happened in the human mind and then got manifested into real life. However, as more systems, we continue to create the more complex our lives seem to have become. Everything subtle and simple is slowly losing its sheen. The systems were created to make our life easier so we could transact with ease, not to make it more complex.

The world is always divided into the haves and the have-nots, luckily the haves are starting to outnumber the have nots which is great news. We must remember always, for everyone to be happy, everyone must be happy!

The saint was quite as the friends sensed this as an opportunity to ask him about those things that were bothering them.

What do the four animal symbols really represent?
They represent the four pillars that support our life, in a way you could call them the four dimensions through which life manifests itself.

i. The **Physical Dimension** is represented by the lion since it has qualities of physical strength and resilience. Often known as the king of all wildlife, it is seen as royal, beautiful, strong, and dangerous. Lions have always been seen as symbols of not only strength but also pride, bravery, and rule. At the same time, the lioness represents the Great Mother which protects its children.

   From Vishnu's avatar known as Narsimha to the ten-armed warrior goddess Durga, you would find reference to the lion in the Hindu Mythology. In fact, the memorial pillar at Sarnath which was erected by Ashoka after his conversion to Buddhism contains four beautifully carved standing lions at the top of a round abacus representing the imperial power.

ii. The **Mental Dimension** is represented by the elephant since it has the qualities of divinity, abundance, fertility, intelligence, keenness, and very strong grasping power. The Ganesha, the lord of the Shiva Ganas, has the head of an elephant and his large head symbolizes knowledge, intelligence, and thinking power. In fact, in the past, there have been dynasties that have been named after the elephants. His trunk represents grasping power, while his big ears denote his attentiveness.

iii. The **Emotional Dimension** is represented by the tortoise/turtle since it has the qualities of, steadiness, patience, stability, wisdom, security, and most importantly love. The tortoise wisdom comes into our lives with the vibrations of peace and tranquillity. Moving gently on the earth reminds us of the essence of self-love. Therefore, it helps you make more meaning to various life experiences that you are currently undergoing. According to the Vedas the form of the god Vishnu's second avatar, Kurma, is a great turtle, which provides a celestial foundation upon which a mountain is balanced.

Being emotionally well is typically defined as possessing the ability to feel and express human emotions such as happiness, sadness, and anger. It also means making effective decisions by integrating feelings, thoughts, behaviours, values, and desires. Emotional wellness encompasses optimism, self-esteem, and self-acceptance. The tortoise symbolizes that emotional wellness.

iv. The **Spiritual Dimension** is represented by the snake since it has the qualities of receptiveness, grace, and healing nature. There is no Indian temple without a snake. One aspect of it is symbolism because, in yoga, a coiled-up snake symbolizes kundalini. But the reason for this symbolic status is because when celestial beings – those who are in consciousness and capability superior to human nature – entered this dimension of existence, they always took the form of a snake. They have been mentioned in every mythology on the planet. In India, there are innumerable stories, starting from Shiva being a Naga Bhooshana. Spirituality is a certain dimension of perception and the snake has come endowed with that capability. That is why the highest form of perception, which is the opening of the third eye in Shiva's forehead, is punctuated by the presence of the snake. If one becomes very meditative, the first creature which is drawn towards that is a snake. This is the reason why you always see images of sages and seers with snakes around. It has such a sense of perception that it can perceive certain dimensions which human beings are longing and desperate to know.

The snake is the first creature that will know even the slightest fundamental change that happens on this planet because his whole body is in touch with the ground. He has no ears; he is stone-deaf, so he uses his whole body as an ear.

A life of balance is a life when we learn how to manage each of these dimensions within ourselves like a professional doing his/her job with utmost precision. People who don't know how to manage their body, mind, and emotions are bound to struggle because you would come across all these situations in your life that would appear like problems simply because you haven't learned how to manage them. These would not be obstacles that life would throw at them; it would be those that you create for themselves.

Life does not give us a choice when it comes to choosing what situations should come our way and that is how it needs to be. Imagine if you could choose exactly what situations would come your way, what a vanilla life it would be. All the mystery surrounding this beautiful life would be sucked away. Therefore, don't ask for easy situations, ask for a more balanced you. Because people who have a certain sense of balance within them can choose to respond to every situation consciously. Unfortunately, most of us, however, never seem to witness this kind of balance inside of us, therefore rather than giving a conscious response to a situation, we give a compulsive reaction. Haven't you seen people who snap out at the smallest of issues? Or people who pick up a habit and cannot give it up, going in compulsive circles, even though they know that habit is not good for them.

Also you must understand that every situation that happens to us can be viewed as either a crisis or an opportunity. If we look for an opportunity in every challenging situation, we would be able to harness our true potential and would be able to grow from strength to strength. On the contrary, if we view every challenging situation as another crisis looming large on our life then we would limit their exposure to life and start to withdraw into our little cocoon.

And no matter how safe that cocoon is, you would not like the butterfly to go back into that shell. We must not only give ourselves the freedom to fly but the courage to express ourselves freely without thinking too much about the consequences. The problem is, once we begin to withdraw from the life we would think twice before committing to anything new. Before anyone realizes, we would have shelved our wings.

How do we apply these learnings to our life?

Balance

Everything you see in nature, exists together, in a delicate balance and if we usually disturb any one element, then all the other elements get interrupted in the entire system. You would have heard that working with plants can improve concentration, encourage relaxation, and improve self-esteem. Digging in rich, black soil just feels good. But why? There is a depth of mystery in the natural world. It is astonishing to witness the healing power of nature. Experiences in nature help people embrace their journey of self-discovery. Nature can open the door to our innate intelligence, awaken the sacred within, and help us to see that everything is connected with a shared purpose, rhythm, but most important a certain sense of balance. Our entire solar system sounds like it must have been set up in a delicate balance – a precisely orchestrated cosmic dance if you will – from the very beginning. Move any piece and it throws the whole solar system fatally out of kilter.

Therefore, it is almost imperative that our life as well its various dimensions would also work at its best when it is in balance. Our body, mind, emotions, and life energies need to be in balance with this cosmic universe because after all, we are nothing but a very small part of this universe itself.

The same applies to those faculties that support our life; one must not exist without the other: Money without intention, Action without purpose, Success without humility, Failures without lessons.

Anything that is not in balance is not in sync with

the very nature of existence! Therefore, once you would understand the power of balance you would not seek anything else.

We want to understand how does this affect some of the most important aspects of life?

Nishant: Work Life Balance
In a true sense, as the saying goes, it is best when you understand that work and life are not separate, it's all life.

A lot of people interpret this in a way that their work becomes their life, while that's not the point. Life is a much bigger phenomenon than what could be captured in your work cubicle. Most people forget about living because they are far too busy trying to make themselves worthy of the materialistic possessions that money could buy. Think about it, when was the last time you saw the evening sun holding a glass of coffee or noticed a smiling face of a child. Our life has become so much more structured and we can certainly boast of ourselves as the most comfortable generation ever, but the question is can we also claim to be the happiest?

Technological advancements have certainly eased our lives but at the same time, they have also filled our life with distractions.

The social media distraction is perhaps the biggest of them all, we all know that it is a boon or a bane provided the way we utilize it. We all know the tremendous opportunities that these platforms provide to us to spread our voices across the globe. Today you could easily sit comfortably within the four walls of your bedroom and speak to the entire world. This power was never available to any other generation except ours. The problem arrives when it starts consuming a majority of our time just into social chit-chat and making videos. This craving for attention is too much for everyone and when the world does not respond to us in the way which we expect, we start getting depressed. If only we realize that through the power of balance, we could utilize social media for any benefits and take away the social distraction completely out of the equation. As human beings you must realize that as a life, you are complete, you don't need any stamp of reference from this world.

On the other side of the road, professionals today are running after success like anything, however, the definition of success is completely connotated in their heads. Success for today's generation means tons of money, cars, and houses to showcase to the world like a piece of trophy. However, if you pay a little more attention to this life, you will realize that this cannot be further from the truth. There are very few millionaires today that could truly claim that they are in a happy space in their life today. If you were to sit with these lucky few and ask about their definition of success, you are likely to hear:

- ✓ Enrichment in relationships both with friends and families.
- ✓ Contributions to the world through their charities as well as the commitment of time.
- ✓ Fulfilling challenging new goals which pushed me away from my comfort zone.
- ✓ Learning something new every day to become a better

version of myself.
- ✓ Travelling the world for amazing new experiences.
- ✓ Exchanging inciting new ideas with people across the globe, understanding their culture and languages.
- ✓ Gaining new experience with music, art, and sports.
- ✓ New adventures especially alongside my loved one.
- ✓ Associating myself with a purpose that I am passionate about.

If you closely observe the above points, you will notice that there is no mention of wealth in terms of money, but without its support, you will find it difficult to fulfil most of the above success parameters. Money gives you options to explore life in true length and breadth, but it cannot be an end goal, if anything it can be only the means to the end.

Amar: Becoming Parents
This is perhaps the single biggest blessing for any two human beings, to be able to come together and bring another life into this world. This blessing though brings along its own set of responsibilities. As parents, you are responsible for the upbringing of your children who are clean slate when they enter this planet. You have the power to mould their life just like craftsman moulds the clay to create new objects.

In my view, every parent must strive to ensure that their child's life is both beautiful, as well as meaningful at the same time. Being beautiful means that they are a true expression of joy and not those who are in pursuit of happiness. At the same time, being meaningful means that they don't waste away their lives before understanding the true nature of this life and have some purpose to strive towards which is not some God-given but something that means something to them.

The problem however is that most of the parents have been conditioned by society in a way that restricts their thinking, rather than empowering it. What is the conditioning that is talking about here?
- Work hard, look for a safe job and keep your head down.
- Taking too much risk is detrimental, play it safe.
- Money is the root of all evil.
- The world out there is filled with selfish and insensitive people.
- Your dream must match your reality.
- Being angry, frustrated is alright, it comes along as a package.
- Keep adjusting to the situations that come along in your life, learn to live within your means.
- Stress is part of our lives, learn to manage.
- Life is hard, accept that.
- It's alright to blame others for your failures: society, economy, company, the government, your bosses, business partners, family members, etc.

This and many beliefs that they harmlessly pass on their children without understanding the likely impact it would have in shaping up their lives. With this kind of mindset, these children are unlikely to strive towards a beautiful and meaningful life. Therefore, it's about time that parents, start to pay attention to how these four dimensions affect our lives. Because when we begin to understand the tremendous impact one could have as parents if we bring about some balance, we could strive to work towards that goal. Bringing about balance could mean a 360-degree change in our approach towards life. Think about passing on these empowering believes to your children instead of the restricting ones:

- Your life is your own making, with the right approach as well as intent, no goal is beyond your reach while striving to fulfil your personal and professional ambitions, think in terms of experiences, growth, and contribution.
- When you empower all your dimensions including the physical, the emotional, the mental, and the spiritual, you could transform yourself completely.
- You owe it yourself, to be happy, joyful, and loving.
- Money as a resource is not evil, the greed for money is.
- Situations would come, situations would go, you always have a choice to consider a situation as an opportunity or a crisis.
- From compulsive reactions to conscious response, that is what you must strive towards.

Your one step in the right direction as parents could transform the lives of your children completely. This is something you owe to them and certainly, you own it to yourself.

Rahul: Earning Money
Earning money for fulfilment of one's desire has been perhaps the greatest enemy of mankind. Millions of people have lost their lives in wars, battles during the time of the empires, all of them after the treasure of wealth.

In today's world people are killing each other for money, gold, and property; nothing much has changed in the way humans behave when it comes to issues involving money. We may call ourselves the most evolved creatures on this planet, however, our attitude towards money is yet to evolve. We still perceived money to be the most important thing in our lives, something without which our lives are incomplete.

Money is simply an idea or instrument which expands our capabilities to do more in this world. Having more money simply gives you more options to perform certain activities which otherwise may not have been possible for you. Your identification with money is really important because if you identify with it in a fallacious way, you run the risk of letting it ruin your life. Far too many people have fallen prey to this greed for money, something which was a means became an end for them.

I know that when you operate in a social setup you need money to run your home, your business, maybe your lifestyle, the trouble starts when money starts running your life. How many examples do we know of people who have themselves ended their life simply because they lost some portion of their wealth? This was because they identified so deeply with their cars, homes, and their lifestyle that they lost perspective of life itself.

I am not someone who is against earning money; In fact, I would encourage people to earn enough for themselves so that they don't have to worry about their survival process. And then anything that we should earn which is over and above our survival process should be used in some way to make a difference to other people's lives. There have been many great saints, intellectuals, business people who have walked this planet having done some great work for not just themselves but also everyone that they have touched, simply because they had the money to make it work. People start associating with money as an emotion; instead, you must look at it as a tool, a tool to provide solutions to the many problems that prevail in this world.

Please understand the importance of tools in our lives. We were able to overcome the biggest obstacles as a human race only because we had the necessary tools to support us. Imagine trying to open a machine without a screwdriver using your hand or teeth, not a good experience right!

Therefore, money in the pocket is not a problem, the trouble starts when it starts getting into your head. The best way to approach money is to have the right identity being attached to it, a daily reminder perhaps that all this money that you own is yours alright, but it cannot be called as you. Every morning first thing, remind yourself about your mortal nature, remind yourself about the purpose for which you are earning this money, and at night try to keep it aside before your sleep. All this would help you identify the right way with money.

Nishant: Taking a Spiritual Path
Just far too many people who have tried to walk the spiritual path find themselves being drawn away from it due to social pressure. The moment you mention to your loved ones that you are on a spiritual path trying to make some meaning for this life, they get worried for you instead of being happy. This is because society has labelled spirituality as a taboo that is reserved only for those who wish to stay in the jungles or ashrams. According to society today these people wear orange or red robes, mostly have their head shaved off or grow a long beard. They think the path of spirituality is reserved for only a few people who are willing to sacrifice all their social life to pursue some stigma.

However, this thought process could not have been further from the truth. Being spiritual is a longing for every human life, it's just that most people do not pay enough attention. They instead try to balance this longing for something by purchasing more fancier assets like jewellery, cars, or houses.

Do not get me wrong, I have no grudges against anyone collecting these assets, however, it's important to know their place in life. The trouble starts when you start becoming dependent on these assets and instead of owning them, they start owning you. The path to spirituality is the path to detachment. The youth of today like you, have the onus to help bring spirituality into our everyday lives. The path of spirituality does require you to give up everything and travel anywhere to an ashram or a jungle but essentially, it's a journey within. It starts with a basic understanding, something that our Vedas and Upanishads have been saying for ages, 'Your life is your own making.'

This essentially means that there is not anyone sitting out there in the sky who is governing your life, you are in fact the one in charge. It requires from you to pay attention to this piece of life that we are first, the life which has been lost behind the shades of becoming a professional, a father, a mother, a student, a husband, a wife, and all the other roles which we play. The physiological drama which plays in our head every day shuns out the inner voice which identifies us as a piece of life. You must understand and ask yourself, why is this important?

You see the more we identify with all the different roles that we play, the more we move away from our source of creation. Instead, if we take on one single identity, which is a piece of life itself, we can easily create a distance between ourselves and the roles that society expects us to play. Please don't take me as wrong; in no ways am I implying that these roles are not important or that we must move away from these social responsibilities. I want you to be completely involved while you perform your duties but at the same time create a certain distance between yourself and these roles that you play daily. It's important to create this distance because not only you would not get entangled, it would help you gain more clarity.

This is like the time when people were confused about whether this planet is round or flat, for years on people debated on this topic with each side giving its reasoning. It was only much later when we developed a spaceship that pivoted high away from the planet that we found the answer. Thus, distance brings a certain kind of clarity. Similarly, when we are too occupied with our daily chores it becomes difficult and often impossible to gain some perspective. We are too busy to take out some time to understand if we are performing our roles well; the basis of self-analysis as well as the feedback loop is closed. It's only when a loved one gives us feedback that we realize that we were doing it all wrong or we were somehow not meeting the expectations. On the other hand, if you give yourself a certain distance, you are much more prepared to learn, adapt and grow within your role.

Let me give you another perspective to understand this. When you ask people as to what is life for them, they would give you all kinds of answers, some would say my children are my life, some would say my work is my life, few in this world also say that my wife is my life. But we all know that is not true, it is just that people identify so closely with their roles as a parent, professional, or husband that their life starts circling these identities. Real life which is the one thriving in each one of us loses its value. The path to spirituality helps you bring this clarity you need to differentiate between what is life and what are the faculties that support life. Armed with this clarity you can be involved yet detached. This is important for people to understand because the majority of the population still thinks that spirituality is something that disempowers them, whereas the exact opposite is true.

Spirituality is Empowerment!

It empowers you by giving you the clarity to proceed in life as well as helping you build up the necessary faculties so that no matter what situation life throws at you, you remain unfazed. Most of the people in this world are afraid to take the next step because they fear that it would bring discomfort to them. Whereas if you have fixed this life in a way that no matter what life throws at you, you are ready then you could simply go on carrying out more and more activities without being worried about the end consequences. Your level of activity in this world is not curtailed in any way by your fear of being in discomfort.

This is like when you want to become an entrepreneur but fear that there are just many factors which not under your control: the market, the economy, the financial constraints, the competition, and many more. However, when you understand that all these situations would play out eventually just like they have played out for everyone else, you could gain some perspective about your approach. Instead of thinking about controlling every factor which plays its part, you could simply focus on what you need to do to get this company running. Find a great problem to solve, develop a service/product that solves that problem, work through with a team to develop that product/service, and market your offering to the right audiences. Now if you would ask the entrepreneurs if the entire journey is as simple as it's been mentioned here, they may not agree with you, however, they would always tell you that the two most difficult decisions were the ones to begin as well as one to keep going. Once you begin, you would realize that success in the business is not a straight line, it passes through many dungeons and passages which test your patience as well as mental aptitude. They require resilience, self-belief, and a certain kind of flexibility to ascertain the conditions to make necessary changes.

All in all, it brings along challenges that help build up your character and shape up your personality. Somebody who understands that these challenges are part of the journey, somebody who takes all the blows on the chin, somebody who does not let what's happening outside, bother them inside, can navigate through these challenges much more swiftly. Your ability to create a distance between you like a piece of life and you as an entrepreneur would help you see more clearly as you navigate these challenges.

Therefore, instead of taking them personally and being consumed in the emotional overdrive, you could simply give out a conscious response. This conscious response would come only when you have a certain sense of balance within you. This applies to any role you play either as a professional or as a parent. No matter what role you are playing in life, just remember these golden rules:

- ✓ Your life is your own making; there is no one up there navigating it for you.
- ✓ Create a certain distance between the various roles you perform as a professional, parent, or wife and yourself as a piece of life. This distance would give your clarity to proceed.
- ✓ Clarity is a poor substitute for confidence, with the clarity you could be involved yet detached.
- ✓ Do not try to control every situation that is happening around you; just fix yourself so that no matter what situations life throws at you, you are just fine.
- ✓ Remember spirituality is a journey from a compulsive reaction to a conscious response.

Amar: Personal Health

Let me tell you a story. A saint was passing through a village where he saw a man offering something to his child, for a moment the saint stopped to observe. On one hand, the man held candy and on the other hand a hundred rupees note. When the man asked the child to choose and the child went for the candy and ran away.

'Stupid isn't he, could have got a hundred candies with this money but he chose the candy instead,' said the man looking at this saint.

The saint came closer to the man and asked him to choose from his hands too, 'On one hand is a crore rupee and on the other hand in your health, you can only choose one my friend, which one would you choose.'

If I offered a similar hand to your three friends as well, what would you choose? The unfortunate thing is that in real life people often choose money over their health, not knowing that if they have their health intact; they could earn much more.

Also, for most people, the definition of health is restricted only towards their physical health so that they could stay away from any illness or disease. However, the definitions of health as we know it needs to change in the people's mind, they need to adopt a more holistic approach while dealing with health.

What is 'holistic health'? The word holistic is defined as: 'characterized by comprehension of the parts of something as intimately interconnected and explicable only by reference to the whole.' So, when we use the word about our health, what we mean is the picture of health that includes not only the obvious physical factors, but mental, emotional, social, and even spiritual factors as well.

In today's modern world, many of our systems and customs seem to be organized in a way that separates the different facets of health – for example, a nutritionist might recommend ways to eat healthfully, and a therapist might recommend ways to cope with stress, but often, there is little to no crossover guidance or framework for fitting the pieces together as a whole.

It seems that we have forgotten the idea that health encompasses not just the absence of physical disease, but involves healthy habits, thoughts, coping mechanisms, and peaceful ways of relating to our environment and to others.

A healthy mind resides in a healthy body. Health is not just physical but mental as well. And one cannot be mentally healthy if one is not physically healthy. Having an unhealthy lifestyle would add to the stress that one already has in his/her life be it work or relationship whereas being healthy would help us in thinking clearly and understanding things better. At the same time, you must also understand that health is not an absolute constant, it keeps navigating between variables. This means while you may be healthy now, there is no guarantee that you would remain healthy after a couple of hours. With that in mind, you must look at the subject of personal health with a certain open mind in the sense that a lot of people who may be appearing healthy from outside, may not be healthy from inside and therefore one must pay attention to those variables which affect personal health. Asking these questions to yourself would go a long way to ascertain if you are paying attention to your health:

- ✓ Do you pay attention to the kind of food you consume?
- ✓ Do you monitor those days when you feel extra energy thanks to the certain food you have consumed?
- ✓ Have you given a thought to the food you are consuming if it's live food or dead food?
- ✓ Do you ascertain the amount of time certain food items stay within your system?
- ✓ Are you monitoring your consumption for stimulant items like tea, coffee, energy drinks, etc.?
- ✓ Are you aware of those food items which are high in proteins, vitamins, and minerals?
- ✓ Do you engage in some kind of physical activity every day?
- ✓ Do you monitor your daily thoughts to sense if there are more empowering thoughts or disempowering thoughts that come across your mind?
- ✓ Do you have some time of the day chalked out to self-analyse your daily routine?
- ✓ Do you have a morning ritual that helps kick start your day with purpose, belief, and confidence?
- ✓ Do you have goals that challenge you to become a better version of yourself every day especially in terms of your health?
- ✓ Do you have the right people surrounding you who constantly encourage you and demand more from life?
- ✓ Are you obsessed with self-growth, learning and developing?
- ✓ Do you listen to the right people, be it family members, friends, mentors, people on television, or social media?
- ✓ Do you have a strong social group for support and guidance?

Remember that your health is your responsibility; it cannot be something that you outsource to the medical industry. Today the western countries spend billions of dollars in supporting the health infrastructure for their people. The pharmaceutical industry is one of the three biggest industries in the world. People today in fact take pride in knowing their family doctors so well, the kind of relationship they have with their doctors is not something they have even with their family members, thus the name family doctors.

You must understand that the medical business should only start when everything else has failed like major surgery or procedure. For everything else, you should be in a precautionary mode. Therefore, instead of running to the doctors or gulping in pills for every small happening, you should instead spend time analysing your daily patterns by answering the above questions.

Always remember, your health is in your own hands, always take utmost attention to it. Wealth is only meaningful if you can share and also enjoy while you are still alive, kicking and healthy.

How do we attain to that level of Balance in our Lives?
Balance is what gives you this power that is talking about, once you are balanced then you can pass through your life completely scratch less as if nothing can touch you. It's as if no storm is big enough and no hurdle is tough enough. On the contrary, if there is a lack of balance you may always be scratching and falling back to your compulsive behaviours.

One thing though that you must understand is that

our life is filled with dichotomies that are constantly trying to pull us away to either corner, we just need to somehow find within us some way to manage these dichotomies. Picture this:

- ✓ When you start running away from death you would escape life!
- ✓ The only thing certain in life is uncertainty!
- ✓ The pursuit of happiness would always bring you unhappiness!
- ✓ The more vulnerable you are, the stronger you appear!
- ✓ The more you learn, the more you realize how little you know!
- ✓ To gain interest, appear uninterested!
- ✓ The only constant thing is change!
- ✓ Leading a highly intricate life, one starts craving for a simpler one and vice versa!
- ✓ The more uncomfortable situations you face, the more comfortable life you ultimately lead!
- ✓ The more money you make, the more you want to make!

Many more…………

So, the challenge arrives, between these dichotomies which one should you choose. Let's understand and observe these dichotomies closely starting from the first one because it would answer for all others.

When you start running away from death you would escape life!

We were given this life so we could experience it to the fullest, now imagine someone too afraid to step out because that person is afraid to die. Well, death would come to that person eventually, maybe after ninety years, but what miserable ninety years those would be. Now imagine the same person instead, choosing to peak his energies to a level where he could just go out there and experience his life to the fullest. Now even if this person only lives for forty-five years, he/she would have lived many a lifetime.

Please understand that your life is never measured in the number of years that you spend on this planet, it is measured on two factors:
I. Intensity of Experience
II. Significance of Impact

Intensity of Experience

The more intense is your experience of life, the more memories you create on your way. Just far too many people have dreams for themselves that have been borrowed from this society. Instead of spending time and energy creating more profound experiences for themselves, they start accumulating assets to show them as some kind of trophies that they have earned. In the process of this accumulation, they forget to live their lives.

Do this much when you guys go back to your life tomorrow, make a list of things that you think would enhance your experience of life. This could be those long vacations that you are planning to go, the pet which you were planning to bring home, the singing or dance lessons you were planning to attend, the public speaking competition you were planning to compete in, the small kids in the poor neighborhood you were planning to teach, the NGO you were planning to associate with, the YouTube channel you were planning to start, basically the new life you were planning to live!

After you have made that list, please do yourself a favour, just go ahead and do it. Not because I am telling you to but because you owe this much to yourself. Once you start making these experiences come to life, you would start noticing remarkable things happening in your life. It would open the flood gates for more such experiences which would automatically come along your way. It was like a chain that was connected to all the doors, once you open one door, the others automatically follow.

Significance of Impact

You must understand that the times we live in today are perhaps most conducive in terms of the scale of impact we would like to have on this world. Never before did we have the resources to speak to the entire world just sitting in our bedroom, but today it's possible provided you had the right intentions and take appropriate actions.

Do note this, the right intentions aren't enough, your intentions need to be backed up by action. But you must also keep in mind that every action that we perform in this world is a direct reflection of who we are. Therefore, if you would like your actions to have a larger impact on this world, you must change your inner experience in some manner.

You would have observed that those people who are naturally joyful by nature find it easier to mix in any environment, the flexibility to adapt to changes, the energy to work for longer hours, the efficiency to produce better results, the persistence to go through hardships, the focus to learn easily, the confidence to think big and most importantly the clarity to get what they want from life.

If you think that all of this is a mere coincidence, then you must think again. Today western science is beginning to realize the importance of being blissful, being kind, and being in gratitude, but eastern teachers have always known them as essential components of a successful human being. The difference is that western philosophy and teachings have always focussed on 'what to do', whereas eastern philosophy and teachings have focussed on 'who we are.' For us, working on ourselves was always imperative since we knew that all human experience essentially happens within us. And our actions in this world are directly linked to the way we experience this world. Positive experiences would lead to positive actions and negative experiences would lead to negative actions, period!

People though always fear losing themselves in the process of trying to create an impact in this world. They fear that the more activity they perform in this world, the more stress, pain, fear, and suffering it would bring to them. If you are also one of them who think like that, then now would be a good time to understand detachment. There is a beautiful definition of the word detachment in the Bhagavad Gita which says that:

'Detachment does not mean that you don't own anything, it means that nothing owns you.'

Krishna says, 'he is the same in pleasure and pain, cold and warmth, victory and defeat for he is detached.'

So, what does that mean? Detachment refers to a higher power. It's the ability to look at things without being affected by pain and pleasure. At the same time, it also means being completely involved with everything you do without really getting entwined.

So, when you question yourself about the process of obtaining total balance within yourself, there are some important components of the process which you must keep in mind.

Your Rituals

You are nothing more than the rituals that you perform every day. Your dreams give rise to your goals, your goals give rise to your plans and your plans give rise to your rituals, that is the process. Therefore, if you want to make something happen you must focus on your daily rituals, in turn, you must focus on the process. In short, your dreams would be a manifestation of your daily rituals. Just far too many people are obsessed with their goals; rather they must be obsessed with the process. If you do the process right, goals will happen as an outcome.

Also, it's important that your rituals connect you with your higher values. These are values like integrity, gratitude, abundance, creativity, kindness, love, compassion, joy, contentment, and many more.

The moment you start these rituals which connect you with your higher values, the quality of your life automatically starts getting enriched. This also means to start to appreciate your life more thereby naturally making more efforts to enrich this life. If you are confused just go back to the four dimensions we talked about earlier. The best way to enrich this life is to consciously start working on each of these dimensions. Create that ritual that enriches each of these dimensions. For example, for your body, look towards healthy eating, exercise, and meditation.

Embrace Change

You would notice that the moment you start making transformative changes in your life, there would be a side of you that would resist this change. That's because you fear the unknown, the present place where you are in something that you have seen, and you are well versed with the settings. But the place which is at the other side of change is still unknown; there could be a thousand different challenges that we may have to face and thus the resistance. However, the truth if that change is always happening, that is how you grow. Celebrate it as it means there are always new things on the way.

The trouble with human beings is the moment they move away from their compulsions they start feeling miserable. It could be unhealthy food, a favourite TV show, morning coffee, or even sex. Engaging in these activities occasionally is not a sin; however, over-indulgence is a problem. Too many people become dependent on these compulsions and start thinking that your life is incomplete without them and this has continued for years. The moment you introduce a new way of life, naturally there is going to be resistance. However, you must not fight this change; you must embrace it with an open mind because if you do you would start to notice that makes your life so much easier. When you are no longer bound by any compulsions, you would start enjoying the freedom which you have never felt before.

Support Circle

Seek mentors and like-minded friends who are on the same course as you are. A journey always becomes more fulfilling if you find companions to come along. Any journey on self-improvement is a time of expansion and surrounding yourself by supporting, co-operating and compassionate people helps to nurture you to grow. Traditional viewpoints and values are changing within many of you and knowing you are not alone are comforting and reassuring.

If you are concerned about your family and friends, whether they would understand this part of your life or not, please know that they don't need to understand what you are up to, however, when they see the transformation within you that they would want to know more. In fact, the best present you can give to your loved ones is to be the best version of yourself.

Evaluate Your Decisions

We are where we are because of the decisions that we make in our lives. Therefore, when you take a deeper look into the choices you are making, you could evaluate the course you are taking. Objective decision-making helps you clear away unproductive energy and that which no longer serves your growth. When you look at things with love, you will see things from a holistic perspective. This means you would certainly not miss the forest for the trees. Your daily choices about your lifestyle, your relationships, the people you would like to associate, your allocation of time would determine how well you can obtain balance within yourself.

The mistake that people make is that they keep thinking about whether this is the best decision in the circumstances, but that is irrelevant. No matter what situation life throws at you, make a choice which you think is in the best interest of everyone, then go ahead and give it your best shot. Don't over think or second guess your decisions, just immerse yourself in the process of making it work, no matter what decision you have made.

Originality

Use your originality and your ingenuity to help you create your desires. Know that any difficult situations will come to an end when you take the time to heal. Be sure to see other's points of view and be open-minded. Review everyone's motives, including your own. Gaining mastery where you help you heal and move on and there are many new and exciting adventures awaiting your arrival.

You don't need to be someone else or better than someone else, the society today has poisoned you with the necessity to become better than the next person. Restrict your competition to yourself and just keep moving forward.

Long-Term Perspective

A lot of people attach wrong expectations when it comes to making change happen in their lives, I am a believer, but I am also pragmatic. I know that meaningful change takes time, it's not a button we can press but at the same time, one must persist with complete faith in the process. What I am asking you here to do is certainly difficult; however, because it's difficult it would take some time, if it was easy it would happen immediately.

Thus, in the short term, there would be temporary hiccups and even failures; however, the belief that the journey is worthwhile should keep you going. Therefore, when you strive, strive for the long run.

You would notice that a lot of the above advice is merely to prepare yourself to become receptive to the possibility of Transformation happening. The more receptive you are to this possibility, the quicker it's likely that the shift would happen.

Where does Success fit in all these?
The saint smiled as he looked at the peaks of the Great Himalayas and paused for a while before speaking. It was perhaps a question which he knew was coming.

The only right thing that perhaps, the so-called Alexander the Great did was the way he chose the last three wishes after he was dead.

1) 'My first desire is that', said Alexander, 'My physicians alone must carry my coffin.'
2) After a pause, he continued, 'Secondly, I desire that when my coffin is being carried to the grave, the path leading to the graveyard be strewn with gold, silver, and precious stones which I have collected in my treasury'.
3) The king felt exhausted after saying this. He took a minute's rest and continued. 'My third and last wish is

that both my hands be kept dangling out of my coffin'.

The people who had gathered there wondered at the king's strange wishes and finally one of them asked him:

'O king, we assure you that all your wishes will be fulfilled. But tell us why you make such strange wishes?'

At this Alexander took a deep breath and said: 'I want my physicians to carry my coffin because people should realize that no doctor on this earth can cure anybody. They are powerless and cannot save a person from the clutches of death. So, let not people take life for granted.

The second wish of strewing gold, silver, and other riches on the path to the graveyard is to tell people that not even a fraction of gold will come with me. I spent all my life Greed of Power, earning riches but cannot take anything with me. Let people realize that it is a sheer waste of time to chase wealth.

About my third wish of having my hands dangling out of the coffin, I wish people to know that I came empty-handed into this world and empty-handed I go out of this world.'

Well, we would never know if this was a true story, but it captures the essence that all good stories would like to portray. Now ask yourself the question, 'Was Alexander the Great a successful man, or was he a failure?'

Countless human beings like Alexander who have walked on this planet have tried to build their definitions of success. For Alexander, the definition of success was perhaps ruling over the entire world. Only on his deathbed perhaps he realized that fallacy was in fact could not have been further from the truth.

One of the biggest evils that mankind has committed is to think that they are here forever. However, we need to raise human consciousness to a level where people should understand that they are all mortal and their time on this planet is limited. With this limited time, they must focus on doing those things that mean something to them rather than running after the success that is driven by society and conceptualized in a greedy mind. However, if your definition of success conceptualizes making this world a better place then you are thinking in the right direction. Since, 'What you do for yourself, dies with you. But what you do for others will live forever.'

This is perhaps the best way to look at success. Let's say you have accomplished everything that you ever wanted to accomplish, you have everything that you ever wanted to have. You have acquired all the toys and assets like the house or a car you always wanted to own, you have travelled the world, established businesses across the globe, moved along with the most powerful people in the globe, would you call your life a success?

You would have read and heard about these people who have achieved all of that and yet at the end of the day they are miserable. When they move about in their social circles, they carry a fake smile on a beautiful face only to show their real feelings when they are alone. The reason that is happening is that they had been chasing an enigma throughout their lives; an enigma which they thought was a success. Now you have been chasing something throughout your life and after having achieved that, you found out that was like a mirage in a desert that never really existed. Now, where do you go? What do you do?

This mirage or enigma is nothing but a definition of success which the society has handed over to us and when someone tries to shift our reality to bring some perspective that the dreams that we are chasing are nothing but phony, we simply walk away from that person thinking they may be jealous.

Therefore, the first thing which you must do is to attach the right meaning to the word success for yourself. Move away from the definition that society has placed on the word success, instead, try, and create your definition by answering some of the most basic questions:

What does the world need?
Look at something that needs to change to make this a better world for all forms of life and not just human life. Just look around yourself, there is so much that needs to change, so many people that need help. It's incomprehensible since all our economies are roaring like anything, but our planet is suffering. We have already consumed half of the resources which are available on this planet and greater than 70% of the world's amphibian species are in decline. Since prehistory, humans have killed off so many species of mammals that it would take 3 million to 7 million years of evolution for them to evolve an equivalent amount of diversity. At least a third of amphibians face extinction, thanks to climate change and habitat loss. And above all, if every human being has to live the same standard of living as American's have today then we would need many more planets.

It's like we are running a huge bus with full throttle, but nobody is holding the steering wheel. And you know what happens when a huge bus runs through like that; it virtually destroys everything that comes in its way. This cannot be the way to live!

As human beings we value ourselves as the most evolved species on this planet, surely, we could learn to conduct ourselves more consciously. Therefore, I am sure you do something that would make this planet a better place to live for us as a generation and for the many generations that are to follow.

So, look around yourself, if you would pay a little attention you would realize what needs to change, pick up the challenge to make that change happen and then completely immerse yourself in the process.

What activity is closest to my heart?
If you have not been able to explore your passions and your interests till the time you are 20 perhaps you never really experimented enough. It is unlikely that you would be able to explore your fascination or zeal sitting inside your four walls watching televisions on Sundays. You need to step out and explore, engage with the people, read books or literature, listen to the world-renowned speakers, that is when ideas would start formulating inside your head.

Watching television is not a problem but just remember this while watching your favourite TV show next time, there are sets of people in that room, the ones inside the glass and the ones which are outside the glass. The ones inside have identified their zeal and fascinations while the ones outside are usually wasting away their crucial productive time. A lot of people feel enslaved to a certain behaviour which they feel then they are not able to break, it could be smoking or drinking, excessive entertainment, wrong eating habits, all of which force them into a corner where they lose their ability to think clearly. Never be a slave to any of these compulsive behaviours which take away your clarity as well as zeal to live.

The way to usually identify your passions is to be childlike, curious to know everything, and joyfully involved in everything you do small or big. Once you are joyfully involved in everything you do, then life would choose for you!

Do not for once ignore this law, yes, it's not a suggestion or an idea, it's a law, just like a law of gravity. Your passions would automatically come to the surface when you joyfully start getting involved in everything you do. People who force themselves wilfully into diverse situations are bound to learn something about themselves that they did not know. Yes, they would test their waters and find out how many strengths they have to endure, most importantly they would find out which situations appealed to them the most during all these endeavours.

Observe yourself during these circumstances, which activity gives you the most joy, and simply do more of that, period!

What are my natural strengths?
Everyone is born with certain instincts which come naturally to them primarily because of their genetic

structure or their environmental conditions or because of some physical labour that was forced upon them. If you have not been able to figure out these strengths, I could suggest that you speak to the people who are closest to you. Ask them about three things that would bet upon you, it could be your ability to communicate that knows the right thing to say in front of the right audience; it could be that you are a natural athlete, it is your compassion or it could your ability to organize.

If you are still unsure about this, maybe it's time you spend some time alone with yourself, away from the noise of this world. Sometimes the only way out to is to look within.

Once you have taken note of your core strengths, you start building a plan around expanding them. The world today is full of people who would tell you that you must work on your weaknesses but you must do the opposite. Spend 100% of the time improving your strengths and when the time comes, lead by your strengths.

And even after you have done everything that has been mentioned above, there are no guarantees that you would be successful in the eyes of this world and that's alright. However, if you are someone who likes to play the probability game then this is something that has the highest probability for you to be a success for this world. You can almost imagine reaching a beautiful place through a tough journey, something like what you have done here. When all these three scenarios align together then you give yourself the best chance to work towards something that's truly worthwhile and perhaps would have reached that beautiful place.

If you are wondering where does earn money fits in this equation, then you again go into survival mode. Please understand that even a small inspect can earn its livelihood and we as a human being with the kind of brains that we have should not be worried about survival. Yes, giving your family a comfortable life is something that everyone wants but does comfort mean gathering all the gadgets around us for entertainment and fulfilment. A penny earned instead to help others is truly worth its value. But it's hard to blame anyone for not understanding this because you are all growing in a society that conditions you to think that success equals money. And this is also because it's the easiest to measure when you compare amongst individuals.

The wealth magazines around the world are busy publishing net worth numbers making the richest people in the world global celebrities. Almost everyone wants to emulate their life, which is natural because that's what you keep hearing and seeing everywhere you go. There are almost no other parameters that measure the success of the individuals apart from net worth.

This definition of success must change now, we must look to thrive and use our wisdom to create a wonderful world around us. A world where the word money naturally does not come into your mind when you call somebody as successful. The only thing that must come to your mind is that this person excelled in his craft and in a way naturally expanded his human potential to create a better world for himself as well as for others. Imagine a world where money is seen only as a platform to transact and where human consciousness is truly valued.

What is more important is that on your last day on this planet you would not have any regrets that I did not do what I could have done. And if there are no regrets then you would surely die as a success, however, I do also wish that your dreams are so big that they take many a lifetime to complete. In that sense, you would have got the ball rolling for somebody to pick it from where you left and keep it going until the final touchdown.

The biggest power is in the realization that you are in charge of the situation, rather than the situation being in charge of you. Once you have come to terms with that, you could naturally respond consciously to anything that life throws at you. Whether it's a loss in business, loss of a loved one, or even something as severe as losing a body part due to an accident or disease, once you know that these are situations that you cannot control, you feel a sense of freedom. Some people describe it as being alive; it's like a moment that you are no longer bound by the compulsions of life. Because whenever you are in compulsions the feeling is similar to going in circles, you may be moving but you are not going anywhere. A lot of people have faced this unfortunate constraint where they feel their life has lost its meaning; it is simply reacting to everything that is happening outside. This is where you need to be conscious and take charge.

In that sense, I bless you that you take charge of these four dimensions and lead your life fearlessly with joy and grace!

A New Chapter!

The three friends waited till the end of the day as the experts from the archaeological survey teams weighed in on the various old books and documents which they found with the treasure. One of the team members came running in towards Nishant:

'This could easily be one of the most prestigious discoveries of our times, sir you have to come and see for yourself. These books and documents were written around the 5th Century it seems and the best part is they are still apparently well-protected.'

Nishant folded his hands to greet the sage asking for permission to leave as he and his friends went in to check.

'Would you like to come in and see all that's inside master,' asked Rahul.

'All that is inside there is already inside me,' replied the master as got up to leave along with his two descendants following him in that black robe.

'Would we ever see you again master?' asked Nishant.

'Remember me and I would come,' replied the master as he turned around to answer before leaving. Not even ten seconds elapsed as the sage disappeared amongst the floating clouds in the Himalayas.

The three friends looked at each other in disbelief for what they witnessed as finally, Amar spoke:

'Do you think he was for real?

'I guess we would never find that out' replied Nishant.

'It feels like we were having a dream, isn't it,' added Rahul.

***

Four Months Later!

The three friends decided to meet at Nishant's place for dinner. Nishant and Isha were waiting for their guests as they stood around at the balcony.

'Are you sure you are not drinking tonight either, this has been like the weirdest four months that I have seen since we have been together?' mentioned Isha as she walked in with a glass of wine as Nishant nodded.

'The story that you have told me about your treasure hunt is starting to feel real because at first, I thought you were just blabbering,' added Isha.

'To be honest it was an experience of a lifetime and the irony is that the best part of the journey did not even involve the treasure' replied Nishant as he smiled while Isha hugged him from behind.

'Have they been able to figure out the values which were there in the treasure?' asked Isha after a brief moment of silence.

'Well the valuables were only used to cover the treasure that was hidden within, that is the books, scientific papers, poems, music notes, and the Vedic literature,' replied Nishant.

'Really?' asked Isha.

'Yea, it's shame that something so valuable in content and enriched with some of the most profound scientific discoveries of the times was hidden away for so long, but the protectors of the treasure did not want it to land into the wrong hands,' added Nishant with a sense of excitement.

Just then the doorbell rang as Nishant moved away from the balcony to open the door. It was Amar and Neha who was there along with their son.

Nishant's son was overjoyed to see his friend and took him away immediately to show him his room while Nishant welcomed Amar as well as Neha.

'Rahul isn't here yet, he seemed to be the one who was most excited about this plan?' asked Amar five minutes after settling down.

'Yea, he mentioned that he had some surprise for all of us, let me just call and check with him' replied Nishant just as the doorbell ringed.

'Finally, you are here, what took you so long?' asked Nishant as he saw Amar standing at the door.

'Shall I be allowed to come in and explain? The reason I came in late is standing behind me,' replied Rahul as he moved into the house holding hands with Kriti.

'Guys this is Kriti,' said Rahul as he introduced everyone. Amar and Nishant looked at each other both surprised and then towards Rahul as they nudged him forward.

'Please come in Kriti,' mentioned Isha as she welcomed all the guests.

'Your surprise is really beautiful Rahul,' added Neha as Kriti giggled looking towards Rahul.

'Hey now that all three of you are together, I have been wanting to ask all of you. What happened during this treasure hunt that changed everything in your lives,' asked Isha.

'Yea so true, both me and Amar have never been happier than we are now. The first thing that he did after he came back was to come to Chandigarh to get us back home. Now he is planning for his nutrition-based start-up' added Neha with excitement.

'Yea and I would show before and after pictures of Nishant in my advertisements. Man, you have lost weight since that adventure, your Zomato friends would be missing you a lot' said Amar smiling as he looked at Nishant.

'Well to be honest he did lose a part of it during the adventure. I still remember him climbing down that rock, remembering his mom on every step-down,' added Rahul as the group erupted into laughter.

'Well, you were equally bad during the time we went underwater. You know Kriti, he would not leave the hand of that lady instructor during the whole time,' replied Nishant.

'Well I am happy he finally dared to walk up to and ask for my hand, that's all that matters to me. Not only that, but he has also gone back to his lifelong passion for writing. Well, the second surprise is that he is writing a book on this adventure of yours' added Kriti as everyone looked at Rahul.

'Wow, so much has changed in these last few months. I still haven't got my answer and I do not want to wait for Rahul's book to learn this. What has brought about this transformation?' again asked Neha.

'Well if can speak for all three of us, it is perhaps those words of the master that still echo inside all the time,' mentioned Nishant.

'The treasure within us is more precious and valuable than any treasure we would find on this planet.'

For a moment there was silence, but you could see

that the three women still had many questions that remain unanswered.

'If you are willing to explore this with an open mind, then allow me to explain,' said a voice which came from the balcony as the group looked outside surprised…....

GOODBYE MESSAGE FROM THE AUTHOR

What is next from here?

Some people like to say that knowledge is power, however, I beg to differ, knowledge is only potential power. Taking the appropriate action in the right direction with intensity and focus based on the knowledge in hand, that's power.

So, if you are wondering, where do I go from here after having garnered all this knowledge, the answer lies in the application. And applying all this knowledge to practice is not easy but it's simple, just like earning money, it's not easy but it's simple. People often use the word simple to suggest something which is just ordinary with no complications, no big problems, but something that is just not interesting. In my view, the word simple is very powerful because if something is simple it means it could be emulated with ease. Something which has a well laid down path and can be learned as well applied with little complications. Therefore, if you would like to become a world-class public speaker you simply need to learn from someone who is already been there and done that, it's that simple.

Learning to be in balance is also simple and with little application as well as some well-drafted techniques you could be well on your way to become the version of yourself that you always desired.

Creating Distance

Distance brings clarity and this clarity is what you would need when life is throwing googlies at you. For e.g., when you are stuck in a traffic jam while getting late for the office or when your office colleague strikes down your next big idea for the ongoing project, or when your business is burning cash as well as losing customers. All these situations would test your balance as a human being and if you want to pass that test with flying colours you would need balance within yourself and the first step to learn anything is to bring clarity in your thoughts. With clarity, you could differentiate between what works and what does not work. And this clarity would come with distance.

Now the question is how do we create this distance?

For years and years, we have been conditioned to identify with these dimensions as ourselves. We cannot simply get up one morning and stop identifying with these dimensions. Therefore, the trick is to give yourself the luxury of time to create this distance.

Your Morning Meditation

Every day, when I sit for meditation in the morning, I repeat in my head again and again that I am not in each of these dimensions. Whatever is not me as a piece of life,

I try and set it aside. And trust me if you do this practice every day then sooner than later you would reach a space where there is absolute clarity. It's like a powerful ritual that you are building for yourself and just like any other ritual it would take some time until it starts showing results, but once you start building the stream, the snowball effect would drive you through.

If you are not someone who is into meditation, just sit comfortably every day for some time in the morning and as you close your eyes, repeat in your head that you are not each of these dimensions. If you would like to make it powerful see yourself travelling like a piece of light outside your body. It's important that you disassociate with your body since it is the most powerful dimension that one identifies with. One of my mentors taught me a powerful light meditation in which he talked about seeing yourself travel as a piece of light to revisit your past, it was a way to heal any negative energies which may be impacting us from the past. And I often use that technique to create the sufficient distance I need within myself. The point is you could use whatever technique works for you, but it's important that you bring clarity within you in terms of your identification with life. We all know that our body is an accumulation of the food that we ate and our mind is made up of impressions that we picked up as we grew up, therefore we must have the necessary wisdom to use them when necessary and to keep them aside when it's not. But if your body or mind starts dictating terms to you then you know there is a challenge. However, the idea here is not to control them in any manner but rather to identify with them in the right way.

The Trigger Technique

Movies have always been a great platform for not just entertainment but some great life lessons as well. If you remember seeing the famous Bollywood movie, 'The Three Idiots,' you would be able to recollect what the actor Aamir Khan would say, whenever he came across a seemingly stressful situation: 'All is Well.'

I honestly believe we all need a trigger, something that reminds us to change our course the moment the situation becomes taxing. That's because a taxing situation often triggers our reptilian mind or in other words as the scientists call the fight or flight response. It needs a trigger for us to remind that this is not a potentially life-threatening situation that we are facing, the fact that instead of the situation being in charge of us, we are the ones in charge.

The trigger which I have developed uses a spiritual pose standing with one hand in front of my body in a lotus posture as I repeat in my head, 'My life is my responsibility and no matter what happens I am in charge.'

Five seconds is all it takes, and your trigger can be anything you choose. Just when life is throwing all these situations at you, just isolate yourself for five seconds and trigger this conscious response. It would be a gentle reminder for you to take charge of the situation. And when you have done this enough times, your mind would automatically learn to respond to every situation in a conscious manner, aka the auto mode.

Lofty Questions Technique

One of the most profound methods or techniques that I found

useful when you are trying to transform yourself is known as the Lofty Questions Technique. It was explained by Vishen Lakhiani in his famous book, "The Buddha and the Badass."

The technique is based on the premise that any transformation essentially starts with an individual alters the way he identifies with himself or herself. This means if you could build an alternative identity about yourself that aligns with your new balanced self which you are trying to build. This is also important since a lot of times we try to bring about transformation through affirmations which often does not work since any forced change in our behaviour that does not align with our identity creates clashes within ourselves.

Therefore, the trick is to build an alternate identity for ourselves. One of the best ways to create an alternative identity for ourselves is through a technique of asking lofty questions. It works because unlike affirmations you are not really making any statements but rather only asking yourself powerful questions. And then you are instructing your subconscious mind to search for answers to those questions. Let me give you a few examples of the Lofty Questions which you could ask yourself:

Why am I so good at creating a certain sense of balance within myself?

Therefore, the key is to ask yourself the all-powerful and empowering question at least once every day in the morning and let the subconscious mind perform its miracle. The way this would work is that your subconscious mind would look for situations in your life that correspond to this behaviour or which vibrate in the same frequency as this expected behaviour and present to you the answer.

Here are some of the Lofty Questions which you must ask yourself every day to build up your life in each of these dimensions:

Physical Health

- ✓ Why do I eat food which is always great for my body?
- ✓ Why do I always take out time for my exercise and physical fitness?
- ✓ Why am I always in a perfect state of physical health?
- ✓ Why is my body healing itself and getting younger as well as fitter every day?

Emotional Health

- ✓ Why am I always surrounded with love?
- ✓ Why am I able to handle failures so amicably?
- ✓ Why do I handle those situations well in which people do not agree with my views?
- ✓ Why am I so good in managing my relationships?

Mental Health

- ✓ Why am I always learning and growing?
- ✓ Why do I never let negative situations overpower me?
- ✓ Why am I never stressed about my work or personal relationships?
- ✓ Why do I always feel that the Universe is conspiring to fulfill my dreams?

Spiritual Health

- ✓ Why do I have such a strong connection with mother

nature?
- ✓ Why do I feel one with this universe?
- ✓ Why do I feel so strongly about all lives on this planet and not just human life?
- ✓ Why am I so motivated always to explore the core of our existence?

The way this technique works is:
Asking Lofty Questions >>> Putting Sub-conscious mind to work >>> Starts looking for answers which synchronize to expected behaviour >>> Starts building your belief Systems >>> More action in the right direction >>> Transformation

Value Entertainment Tool

Your Last Day on This Planet…
A wise man once said 'On your last day on earth, the person you could have become will meet the person you became. I hope you don't regret then.'

On their deathbeds, one of the most important regrets that people have is that they never took the chances they could have taken, they never spoke their heart out to those loved ones, they never visited the places they should have gone and they never lived the life they should have lived.

Are you going to be one of those people?

Just thinking about this should propel you into taking some kind of action to make a change in the way you look at life. One of the things that always works is for us to constantly remind ourselves that we are mortal, the fact that our time on this planet is limited. This reminder serves us well to focus on things that truly mean something to us.

The challenge in today's hyperactive world is that there are some many distractions that one encounters in her day-to-day life that it's difficult to keep the focus on what truly means something to you. Most of these distractions propel you towards entertainment sources that keep you occupied throughout the day without really adding any value.

Therefore, it's very important for you to monitor your daily activities to see if you are taking a balanced approach towards both values as well as entertainment, which I like to call the value entertainment tool.

Value Entertainment Tool

Value	Creative Time	Productive Time
	Vision board – Visualization Sitting in silence to reflect on your day Meditation Calibrating on your goals	Reading books Courses/Videos/Seminars to enhance your skill set Sports, Arts and Music Networking and Collaboration Practicing your skill
	Destructive Time	**Superfluous Time**
	Over sleeping Surfing TV channels Studying without any focus	Social media Video games Overindulgence in alcohol, parties and drugs OTT platforms

Entertainment →

Let's understand what each of these quadrants represents and what portion of your time is ideal for you to spend in these quadrants:

I. **Destructive Time:** The quadrant represents the time that you spend in which neither is there any value-added nor is there any entertainment attached to this.

It's because of pure laziness or lack of interest in any activity that one spends too much time on the bed lazing around or watching television, indiscriminately changing channels. This quadrant deserves zero portion of your daily time unless you are recovering from some illness.

II. **Superfluous Time:** This is the quadrant to look out for, it's like the mousetrap, which is easy to get in, however, the escape route is very challenging. You sit yourself down in front of the TV after a long day at work and decide to start watching that new show everyone's been talking about. Cut to midnight and you've crushed half a season — and find yourself tempted to stay up to watch just one more episode, even though you know you'll be paying for it at work the next morning. It happens to all of us thanks to streaming platforms like Netflix and Amazon Prime. According to Dr. Carr, the process we experience while binge-watching is the same one that occurs when a drug or other type of addiction begins. 'The neuronal pathways that cause heroin and sex addictions are the same as an addiction to binge-watching,' Carr explains. 'Your body does not discriminate against pleasure. It can become addicted to any activity or substance that consistently produces dopamine.'

The University of Texas study found that binge-watchers were more likely to be depressed, lonely, and have less self-control. One of the study's authors, Yoon Hi Sung, Ph.D., stated: 'When binge-watching becomes rampant, viewers may start to neglect their work and their relationships with others.' Another study found that binge-watching was related to poorer sleep quality, more fatigue, and insomnia, because of pre-sleep arousal. Researchers have also found that watching three or more hours of TV a day is associated with premature death.

Now let us take the example of Video Games. Many researchers believe that excessive gaming before age 21 or 22 can physically rewire the brain. Researchers in China, for example, performed magnetic resonance imaging (MRI) studies on the brains of 18 college students who spent an average of 10 hours a day online, primarily playing games like World of Warcraft. Compared with a control group who spent less than two hours a day online, gamers had less grey matter (the thinking part of the brain).

As far back as the early 1990s, scientists warned that because video games only stimulate brain regions that control vision and movement, other parts of the mind responsible for behaviour, emotion, and learning could become underdeveloped. However, violent video games are of concern to many experts. In a study of 45 adolescents, playing violent video games for only 30 minutes immediately lowered activity in the prefrontal regions of the brain compared to those who participated in a non-violent game. Previous research showed that just 10–20 minutes of violent gaming increased activity in the brain regions associated with arousal, anxiety, and emotional reaction, while simultaneously reducing activity in the frontal lobes associated with emotion regulation and executive control.

The larger picture if for us to understand is that it's good to sometimes let our hair down and enjoy outside with friends and family either partying, playing video games, watching a movie together, etc. The concern remains when we overindulge in these things. The results could be catastrophic as have seen in the case of OTT platforms or video games. The bigger concern also is with the fact that the more time we spend on pure entertainment, the further we move away from spending time in achieving our goals and objectives. We would read about this in the next two quadrants but the key to remember is that it's alright sometimes to spend a portion of your time in this quadrant, however, avoid being carried away because you must realize that it's far more rewarding to achieve your potential in real life.

III. **Creative Time:** Everyone needs time for themselves to gather their thoughts as well as to allow the subconscious mind to perform its magic. When you have given a problem to a conscious mind to solve you must allow for it to process for some time without thinking too much about the solution. This essential time can be termed as creative time.

In the book Stillness is the Key Ryan Holiday writes, and I quote, 'Stillness is what aims the archer's arrow. It inspires new ideas. It sharpens perspective and illuminates' connections. It slows the ball down so we may hit it. It generates a vision, helps us resist the passion of the mob, makes way for gratitude and wonder. Stillness allows us to persevere. To succeed. It is the key that unlocks the insights of genius and allows us, regular folks, to understand them.'

As the boss of Microsoft, Bill Gates would take one week, two times a year, and escape by himself to a secret clapboard cabin somewhere in a cedar forest in the Pacific Northwest. It was what he called his Think Week. Work done during one Think Week eventually led Microsoft to launch Internet Explorer in 1995.

Bill Gates' 'week in the woods' idea is smart, says Laura Stack, president, and CEO of consulting firm The Productivity Pro. 'People should have a 'third place' that isn't working or home, where they can find focussed time to think and create and clarify your strategic thinking,' Stack says. 'We must create an environment that gives us the ability to focus our minds without interruption from co-workers, spouses, children, pets, and technology, or we'll never be able to concentrate on higher-order activities.'

Let's move to another story, that of Isaac Newton when he invented gravity. Isolation, self-quarantine, social distancing. Each suddenly has become a daily part of our lexicon as cases of COVID-19 increase across the country. The world has been through pandemics before and will again in the future, but it was during Newton's time the Great Plague of London spread across the city. This was 1665 to 1666, when a suspected 100,000 people died out of a population of only 460,000 people, according to Britannica.

Away from university life, and unbounded by

curriculum constraints and professor's whims, Newton dove into discovery. Without his professors to guide him, Newton thrived. At home, he built bookshelves and created a small office for himself, filling a blank notebook with his ideas and calculations. Absent the distractions of typical daily life, Newton's creativity flourished. During this time away he discovered differential and integral calculus, formulated a theory of universal gravitation, and explored optics, experimenting with prisms and investigating light.

Now people think if they do this it would take away time from their daily tasks. There's nothing wrong with keeping up with daily work. If you're part of a company, keeping up probably means you're pretty productive, and might even earn a promotion once in a while. But here's the thing: you reach a point where keeping up no longer feels like enough.

The more autonomous your work, the more valuable reflection time becomes. Reflecting helps you step back from your work so you can think about new opportunities that are out there, process your challenges, and question what you could be doing differently. It allows us to place the hypothetical rudder with intent, correcting our course so we can travel in a more productive and meaningful direction. The value of reflection applies to all critical areas of our lives. The more you reflect on your work, the more meaning you'll find in it, and the less you'll get caught up on unimportant tasks. The more you reflect on your personal life, the more you'll start noticing and experiencing moments with your loved ones.

Now, let's take the example of meditation and what does it do to our system. Many studies have investigated meditation for different conditions, and there's evidence that it may reduce blood pressure as well as symptoms of irritable bowel syndrome and flare-ups in people who have had ulcerative colitis. It may ease symptoms of anxiety and depression and may help people with insomnia. Some research suggests that meditation may physically change the brain and body and could potentially help to improve many health problems and promote healthy behaviours.

This quadrant serves the purpose of bringing in the much-needed time of solitude to your daily routine which you could well use to invest in yourself. Ideally, it's always preferred that invest this time in the morning, wherein there are hardly any disturbances in place for you. An hour of personal time to meditate, plan, reflect and gratitude is perhaps the perfect start to the day. It prepares you physically, mentally, emotionally as well as spiritually for what lies ahead during the day.

I like to do my Yoga, meditation in the morning followed by spiritual chants as well as morning affirmations. Then I like to spend a few minutes reflecting on the day that just finished to see what my learnings could be and what I need to do better going forward. This is followed by a quick assessment of what lies ahead during the day in terms of the key tasks that I would like to accomplish before the day is finished. Few of things that always find a place in my schedule include:

i. Reading for at least two hours
ii. Spiritual videos
iii. Learning something new
iv. Finding time for my daughter
v. Writing on my upcoming book/article
vi. Important professional tasks

> Now you can completely automate this process if you pay enough attention to yourself as well as your current circumstances. Taking out time for yourself is something you owe to yourself and trust me once you start this process; you would get addicted and would not want to stop.

IV. **Productive Time:** People often come back complaining that they never seem to get anything done throughout the day, even though they seem to be more than busy than ever. This is because they are usually busy doing things that never add any productive element to their schedule. The best way to monitor if you are spending enough time in the productive zone is to monitor if your activity is fuelling your growth engine to propel you towards achieving your life goals. If doing the activity brings you closer to your goal, then please consider the time spend doing that activity as productive.

Another way to monitor productive time is to see if the time spends is in some way growing you intellectually, emotionally, financially, and spiritually as well as increasing your physical or mental fitness. A lot of people often confuse productive time with superfluous

time, these are some of the arguments they make:
- ✓ *I am spending time on Instagram, Twitter, or Facebook for networking.*
- ✓ *I am watching OTT shows to de-stress myself from my tough office routine.*
- ✓ *I am going out to parties because I need to socialize.*
- ✓ *I am watching English movies to increase my command of the language.*
- ✓ *I am playing video games to improve my problem-solving skills, enhance my memory and improve my concentration power.*

We have all heard of these excuses and sometimes even have been party to them to convince ourselves that we have a valid excuse to indulge in superfluous time. However, we all know that no matter what excuse we give, over-indulgence in any of these activities would not serve us well in the long run. Instead, keep yourself focussed on the following productive techniques:

- Dedicate time from your everyday routine to reading books; this is the single biggest differentiator between those who achieve and those who only dream. If books become part of your daily routines especially early morning and late at night, then you would see a remarkable change in your character and personality. Read those books that empower you and challenge you to think beyond your comfort zone. Reading books cannot be just another habit you pick up when you have free time, it must become a necessity in your life.
- Understand that no matter where you go and what you

do, you would have to interact with people. So, the most productive use of your time would be to develop people skills. Also learning a new skill requires you to listen, ask questions, clarify your understanding, and often reinforce new skills in practice with others. The better you are at active listening, asking thoughtful questions of others, communicating clearly, and collaborating with team members — the more likely it is that you'll learn faster and also remember more of what you learned. Here are some of the most prolific ways that you could develop people skills:

I. *Associate with people and exchange ideas with them on every possible opportunity that comes your way.*
II. *Listen to people who have opposite thoughts to help build up an overall perspective.*
III. *Contribution to society is the best way to acquire people skills. Giving your time and efforts towards a cause bigger than yourself is what selfless love is all about.*
IV. *Gratitude and kindness are the two biggest tools that the human race possesses yet they continue to be the most underutilized ones, people that are kind to others just know their way around them.*
V. *People know when you're truly interested in them; Ryan Kahn a career coach puts it best. 'If you're not showing a genuine interest – asking thoughtful questions and considering their answers – your interaction can have an opposite effect to the one intended. Take care to remember names, dates, and important life events.'*
VI. *You must develop a natural tendency to trust others;*

nothing ever gets accomplished as a team unless you learn to trust people.

VII. *Learn to laugh at yourself; a joyful human being is always a wonderful human being. And everyone wants to be around wonderful people. No one would ever opt to be around someone who is grumpy, frustrated, and carries a long face.*

VIII. *People want to work with those that they know they can trust. Honesty is the foundation of any relationship, whether professional or personal. If you are not honest with the people that you are working with, it is unlikely that your relationship would last for long.*

IX. *Everything that comes out of your mouth should be to empower, motivate or encourage someone. Keep your criticism and complaint only restricted to yourself.*

- Make learning a daily habit, incremental gains every day towards your betterment. Any day in which you do not become a better version of yourself is a wasted day. The key is to pick up five things that you would like to better with; it could be your relationships, your spiritual journey, your communication skills. Then instead of just hoping to get better by default design a plan through conscious practice. A conscious practice usually involves the following key elements:
    i. *Short team measurable goals*
    ii. *Always try to better the previous day*
    iii. *Feedback loop*
    iv. *Guidance from mentor*

v. *Try new techniques if you are struck*
vi. *Persistence to go all the way*

- Often the most productive time of the day is spent with reconnecting with those activities that your heart desires. It could be music, arts or sports whatever your area of interest may be, spending time in solitude practicing your violin skills, writing your next poem, kicking the football.

Measure Yourself

If you would like to explore where do you stand in terms of these dimensions, you could simply try and measure yourself by answering some simple questions.

Based on the answers that you provide, you could rate yourself on a scale of one to ten in each of these dimensions. Now the important thing to note is not to get carried away by giving yourself more points so that you could win a popularity contest. Please understand this is a true self-assessment, it would only work if you are truly honest with yourself.

Emotional Questions
I. Do you easily get upset when someone does not meet your expectations?
II. Are you struggling with a loss of a loved one who has left a permanent impairment in your life?
III. Do you often feel overwhelmed when people say something which you disapprove of?
IV. What kind of relationships do you share with the

people in your life, positive or negative?
V. Do you easily get gloomy when things don't go your way?

Physical Questions
VI. Do you maintain a healthy routine of physical exercise?
VII. Do you pay attention to your food intake, in terms of both qualities as well as calories?
VIII. Does your routine include researching the latest best practices on physical fitness?
IX. Do you eat compulsively often due to some stress or tight deadlines?
X. What are your thoughts on Yoga and meditation?

Mental Questions
XI. Do you allow negative feelings to overpower your thoughts often?
XII. Do you consider this world a friendly place or a hostile place to live in?
XIII. Are you often stressed out in your professional or personal space?
XIV. Do you have written down goals and give time to visualizing these goals?
XV. Do you work every day in some way to keep yourselves motivated?
XVI. Do you try to maintain a positive circle of people surrounding you?

Spiritual Questions
I. What does spirituality mean to you, is it about god, religion or is it about exploring the nature of life?
II. How strong is your connection to mother earth?
III. How about your connection with all forms of life on this planet?
IV. Are you currently practicing any spiritual practice?

Now please understand this exercise is merely about exploring new possibilities within yourself, these tests do not determine anything except maybe prompting you to think in the right direction. And with clarity, desire, and commitment you can make the necessary changes in your life that help enrich the experience of your life as well as the necessary impact you can have in this world.

Therefore, promise yourself that you would do everything possible to become better physically, mentally, emotionally and spiritually.

In the End!

There was a beautiful story of 'Gautama, the Buddha' and his disciples.

This was the time when he was trying to spread his teachings far and wide into the various villages of this country.

One day, the Buddha and a large following of monks and nuns were passing through a village. The Buddha chose a large shade tree to sit beneath so that group could rest awhile out of the heat. He often chose times like these to teach, and so he began to speak. Soon, villagers heard about the visiting teacher and many gathered around to hear him.

One surly young man stood to the side, watching, as the crowd grew larger and larger. To him, it seemed that there were too many people travelling from the city to his village, and each had something to sell or teach. Impatient with the bulging crowd of monks and villagers, he shouted at the Buddha, 'Go away! You just want to take advantage of us! You, teachers, come here to say a few pretty words and then ask for food and money!'

But the Buddha was unruffled by these insults. He remained calm, exuding a feeling of loving-kindness. He politely requested that the man come forward. Then he asked, 'Young man if you purchased a lovely gift for someone, but that person did not accept the gift, to whom does the gift then belong?'

The odd question took the young man by surprise. 'I guess the gift would still be mine because I was the one who bought it.'

'Exactly so,' replied the Buddha. 'Now, you have just cursed me and been angry with me. But if I do not accept your curses if I do not get insulted and angry in return, these curses will fall back upon you – the same as the gift returning to its owner.'

The young man clasped his hands together and slowly bowed to the Buddha. It was an acknowledgement that a valuable lesson had been learned. And so, the Buddha concluded for all to hear, 'As a mirror reflects an object, as a still lake reflects the sky: take care that what you speak, or act is for good. For goodness will always cast back goodness and harm will always cast back harm.'

The way Buddha chose to teach his followers about our minds and emotions is precisely the way we need to practice these dimensions.

In 2010, Hank Genaske who was a resident of California was hit by a mail truck while biking along with one of his favourite routes. Despite wearing his helmet, he sustained a fractured skull and endured a year-long hospital stay where he lay in a coma. Initially unable to speak or even swallow on his own, Hank underwent intensive therapy over several years, slowly building himself back up after his traumatic accident. Although he had gained back much of his executive functioning, Hank was told by doctors that he would never be able to walk again. Despite the prognosis from his doctors, Hank began walking every day, walking around the grounds and going up and downstairs to build his strength back up. Eventually, three years after his accident, he was finally strong enough to remove the feeding tube he had received.

A Sunrise resident since 2013, Hank is still dedicated to the exercises that saved his life, starting his day with 100 pushups and 80 sit-ups. He also uses weights to strengthen his arms and has formed a special bond with Buddy, the community dog, whom he takes on 1 1/2-mile walks every morning and evening. An ordinary man but an extraordinary story!

There are millions of such stories of people having lost their body parts or become paralysed but having something inside of them which led to their mysterious recovery. That something inside could be termed as balance!

The most important thing to understand here is that we as human beings can create our own experiences. This means if you would like to find your joy, you should not be dependent on any situation or person. Just far too many people in this world are searching outside for answers to those questions which lie within them. And most importantly just far too many of us blame somebody else for our failures; life works best when you take complete responsibility for it. Period!

With all these powerful techniques, as well as the ability to measure yourself in terms of these dimensions, I am sure you would create a version of yourself that stands tall in no matter situations life throws at you. If life throws stones at you, you will create a palace and if life throws mud at you, you will use it as manure to grow your plant.

Just remember the journey of balance is the journey from compulsive reaction to conscious response. I wish you all the best for this journey and hope to see you on the other side!

ACKNOWLEDGEMENTS

This book is special to me on many different levels and authoring in front of it has been an absolute soul-searching experience. I have tried to imbibe some of these learnings into my life and they have been of immense help. I would encourage everyone to do the same and experience a new version of yourself!

Every outcome in this world is an effort, a lot of forces that combine together in various permutations and combinations to make it work. These forces often operate behind the curtain, not viewed by the audience, but that doesn't make their efforts any less significant. This book too is an effort of a lot of people who have worked with me to educate and encourage me to give my best outcome.

To start this book would not have been possible had someone not knocked on my door and answered my prayers which I needed them to be answered the most. To someone who made me understand the meaning of life and showed me the immense possibility that we have as human beings to expand our potential. He is someone who truly transformed my life and I am sure the lives of many such individuals like me, to my Guru Sadguru Jaggi Vasudeva.

To my wonderful family, who is my pillar of strength, standing behind me in every new endeavour that I throw myself into, never really questioning my intentions, just being there for me especially my mom and my wife. Then to my miracle daughter whom I see every day and be thankful to life for showering me with such a beautiful blessing.

To my publishing partner Sagar along with his amazing team of Anecdote for believing in this book and bringing it to life.

To my very talented and good friend Sumit whose amazing sketch art has given this book the visual finish it deserved.

To a wonderful friend who always encouraged me to write and express myself, gave me the methods as well as the tools along with some great insights into the world of book publishing. A renowned author himself, Kapil Raj.

In the end I would like to extend my gratitude to the readers who make this journey worthwhile as an author by sending in their blessings. They are not only my source of inspiration for writing but also my biggest source of feedback. This acknowledgement is also an invite to everyone who is reading this book to come forward and talk about their experience, share your insights as well as give some pragmatic feedback. Your views mean the world to me, please reach out to here:

varunwadhwa13@gmail.com